ROADMAP A2+

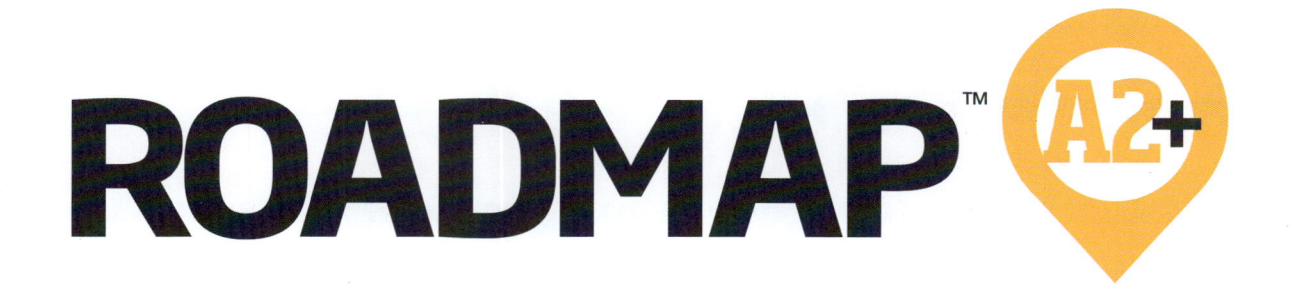

FLEXI EDITION COURSEBOOK 1
with digital resources and mobile app

Lindsay Warwick and Damian Williams

Contents

FAST-TRACK ROUTE

MAIN LESSON	GRAMMAR/FUNCTION	VOCABULARY	PRONUNCIATION	SPEAKING GOAL
UNIT 1 page 6				
1A Getting to know you page 6	word order in questions	question words	intonation	get to know someone
1B Successful people page 8	adverbs of frequency	success	connected speech	describe habits and routines
1C A new lifestyle page 10	present simple and present continuous	everyday activities	contractions	describe everyday activities
1D English in action page 12	ask for and check information			ask for and check information
Check and reflect page 13 Go online for the Roadmap video.				
UNIT 2 page 14				
2A One of those days page 14	past simple	feelings	-ed endings	describe a memorable day
2B You're never too old page 16	past simple negative and questions	past time expressions	did/didn't, was/wasn't	ask about and describe past events
2C Unusual tastes page 18	quantifiers	adjectives to describe food	connected speech	describe a special dish
2D English in action page 20	show interest and excitement			show interest and excitement
Check and reflect page 21 Go online for the Roadmap video.				
Communication game: Four in a row (Units 1-2 review) page 146				
UNIT 3 page 22				
3A Urban escapes page 22	comparatives	adjectives to describe places	weak forms	compare places to visit
3B A place to stay page 24	superlatives	hotels and places to stay	superlatives	choose a place to stay
3C Never ever page 26	present perfect with *ever* and *never*	verb phrases	has/hasn't, have/haven't	describe past experiences
3D English in action page 28	give and respond to news			give and respond to news
Check and reflect page 29 Go online for the Roadmap video.				
UNIT 4 page 30				
4A Special days page 30	*be going to*, *want* and *would like*	celebrations	weak forms	talk about plans for a special day
4B Planning events page 32	*will/won't* for decisions and offers	organising events	contractions	organise an event
4C Rules of the race page 34	*can* and *have to*	-ed and -ing adjectives	sentence stress	present an idea for an event
4D English in action page 36	make plans to meet			make plans to meet
Check and reflect page 37 Go online for the Roadmap video.				
Communication game: Keep talking (Units 3-4 review) page 147				
UNIT 5 page 38				
5A The right person page 38	relative clauses with *who*, *which* and *that*	job skills and preferences	*who*, *which* and *that*	describe a job
5B Appearances page 40	*look like*, *look* + adjective, *be like*	appearance	connected speech	describe people
5C Shopping tips page 42	*should*, *shouldn't* and imperatives	shopping	sentence stress	give advice about shopping
5D English in action page 44	make and respond to suggestions			make and respond to suggestions
Check and reflect page 45 Go online for the Roadmap video.				
Communication game: Roadmap race (Units 5-6 review) page 148				

Grammar bank page 116   Vocabulary bank page 136   Communication bank page 151   Irregular verbs page 160

EXTENDED ROUTE

DEVELOP YOUR SKILLS LESSON	GOAL	FOCUS
1A Develop your listening page 86	understand a short talk	understanding the main idea
1B Develop your writing page 87	complete a questionnaire	explaining reasons and results
1C Develop your reading page 88	understand a short article	reading for specific information
2A Develop your reading page 89	understand a short story	narrative structure
2B Develop your writing page 90	write a story	using adverbs to describe actions
2C Develop your listening page 91	understand a short talk	recognising weak forms
3A Develop your reading page 92	understand a factual text	guessing the meaning of words
3B Develop your writing page 93	write a hotel review	organising ideas
3C Develop your listening page 94	understand an interview	predicting information
4A Develop your writing page 95	write and respond to an invitation	inviting and responding
4B Develop your listening page 96	understand instructions	sequencing words
4C Develop your reading page 97	understand a review	understanding pronouns
5A Develop your reading page 98	understand an article	identifying positive and negative points
5B Develop your listening page 99	understand a short talk	understanding linkers
5C Develop your writing page 100	write a guide	linking ideas

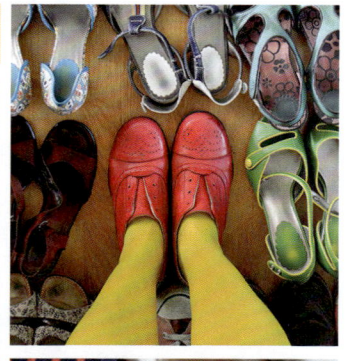

DEVELOP YOUR SKILLS LESSON	GOAL	FOCUS

1A Getting to know you

> **Goal:** get to know someone
> **Grammar:** word order in questions
> **Vocabulary:** question words

Reading and vocabulary

1 **Work in pairs and discuss the questions.**
   1 Do you share information online? What sort of things do you share?
   2 How and why do you share this information?

2 a You're going to read a social media post by Magda. Look at her photos. What topics do you think she writes about (e.g. holidays)?

   b Read Magda's post and check your ideas. Then answer the questions.
   1 Which topics in the post are not in the photos?
   2 Where does Magda work?
   3 Is Abby a good friend?
   4 What do Magda's friends and family not know about her? Why?

3 a Match the question words with the answers.
1	How	a	tomorrow
2	How long	b	a phone
3	How many	c	I like Italian food
4	What	d	two hours
5	What kind of	e	five
6	When	f	that one
7	Where	g	by train
8	Which	h	It's his
9	Who	i	in Los Angeles
10	Whose	j	because I'm tired
11	Why	k	John

Magda Fisher
Yesterday at 21.33

Ten things about me

1 **Where do you like to relax?** At the beach. I love the sound of the sea.
2 **How do you travel to work or college/school?** I walk.
3 **How long does your journey to work take?** About 20 seconds – from my bedroom to my home office.
4 **What's your favourite drink?** Coffee. I have five or six cups a day. Shh, don't tell anyone!
5 **Whose name is first in your phone contacts?** Abby – she's my sister's best friend! **Do you know the person well?** Actually, I've only met her once!
6 **When are you happiest?** When I'm visiting somewhere new. **Why?** Because new places are exciting.
7 **What kind of music do you like**? 1970s rock music. Thanks, a lot, Dad!
8 **Which animals do you like?** Cats, especially my cat Bubble!
9 **How many pairs of shoes do you own?** I've got over 30, but I always wear the same pair of trainers. My family and friends think they're my only shoes – but that's only because I never wear the others!
10 **Who is your oldest friend?** Nina. We have so much fun together. **Are you a good friend to him or her?** I think so ... most of the time!

b Match Diego's answers a–j with questions 1–10 in Magda's post.

   a About five. Who needs more than that?
   b Someone I work with called Alex. I know him quite well.
   c By bike when it's sunny. By car when it's raining.
   d When I'm playing my guitar. I love music.
   e About 30 minutes.
   f At home, in my living room, with some music on.
   g Two people, actually – Sofia and David. We're great friends.
   h Anything with a guitar – rock, mostly.
   i Fresh juice, especially on a hot day.
   j I love horses!

c Work in pairs. Take turns to ask and answer six questions in Magda's post.

Go to your app for more practice.

Grammar

4 a Read the grammar box and choose the correct alternatives.

Word order in questions

Order questions in the present simple like this:
(Question word +) *do* + subject + infinitive
How do you travel to work or college/school?
How long ¹*do/does* the journey take?
²*Does/Do* you know the person well?
Order questions with *be* like this:
(Question word +) *be* + subject
What is your favourite drink?
Who ³*are/is* your oldest friend?
⁴*Are/Do* you a good friend to him or her?

b Check your answers in Magda's post in Exercise 2.

5 a 🔊 1.1 Listen to the questions. Does the speaker's voice go up or down at the end of each question?

  1 What kind of pizza do you like?
  2 Who's your favourite singer?
  3 Where do you live?
  4 Why are you tired?
  5 How long is this lesson?

b Listen again and repeat.

6 a Put the words in the correct order to make questions. Use capitals where necessary.

  1 spend online / you / do / how many hours / each day / ?
  2 who / you / online / talk to / do / ?
  3 look at / whose photos / you / do / online / ?
  4 like / what kind of / do / websites / you / ?
  5 you / this area / from / are / ?
  6 your normal working day / how long / is / ?

b Make questions using the prompts. Choose an appropriate question word or expression.

  1 your birthday? *When's your birthday?*
  2 your favourite TV show at the moment?
  3 films / like?
  4 languages / you / speak?
  5 you / go / at weekends?
  6 this lesson / finish?

c Work in pairs. Take turns to ask and answer three questions in Exercise 6a and three questions in Exercise 6b.

Go to page 116 or your app for more information and practice.

Speaking

PREPARE

7 a 🔊 1.2 You're going to get to know your classmates better. First, listen to Becky and Josh and answer the questions.

  1 How many films does Josh talk about?
  2 Why is Becky surprised?

b Listen again. What questions does Becky ask?

8 Think of some topics that you're interested in and write some questions to ask your classmates.
Do you like sport?
Are you a student?

SPEAK

9 a Work in groups. Take turns to ask your questions to each other. Ask some follow-up questions and use the Useful phrases to help you respond.

  A: *Do you like sport?*
  B: *Yes, I really like football and tennis.*
  C: *Really? Me too! Do you play football?*

Useful phrases
That's interesting/nice.
Really?
Me too!
Great!

b Tell the class one or two interesting things about the people in your group.

Develop your listening
page 86

1A | Getting to know you

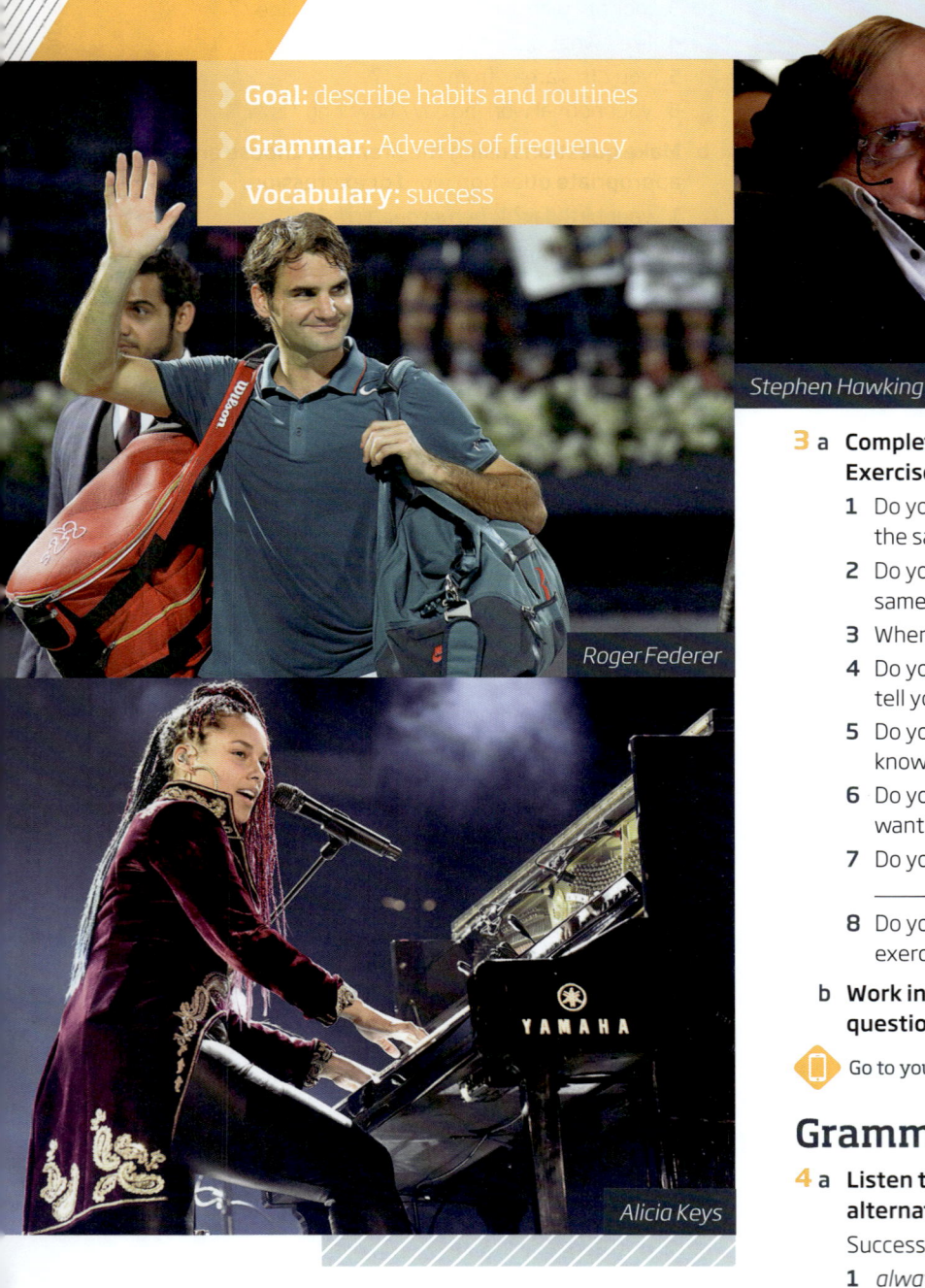

1B Successful people

> **Goal:** describe habits and routines
> **Grammar:** Adverbs of frequency
> **Vocabulary:** success

Roger Federer
Stephen Hawking
Natalia Osipova
Alicia Keys

Listening and vocabulary

1 Look at the photos and discuss the questions.
  1 What do you know about these people?
  2 Why do you think they are/were successful?
  3 What habits do you think successful people have?
    I think they get up early and work late.

2 a ◆ 1.7 Listen to a podcast about successful people. Does it include any of your ideas?

  b Listen again. Number the tips in the order you hear them. Do you agree with them?
   • take care of yourself
   • plan your time well
   • try new things
   • have clear goals *1*
   • take time off
   • start again
   • ask a lot of questions
   • listen carefully

3 a Complete the questions with an expression in Exercise 2b.
  1 Do you _plan your time well_, or do lots of things at the same time?
  2 Do you like to _____, or repeat the same experiences?
  3 When things go wrong, do you _____?
  4 Do you _____ to what other people tell you?
  5 Do you _____ when you want to know something?
  6 Do you _____? Do you know what you want in life?
  7 Do you think it's more important to work all the time, or _____ and enjoy yourself?
  8 Do you _____? Do you eat well and do exercise?

  b Work in pairs. Take turns to ask and answer the questions. Do you have similar habits?

  📱 Go to your app for more practice.

Grammar

4 a Listen to the podcast again and choose the correct alternatives.
  Successful people …
  1 *always/never* know what they want in life.
  2 are *sometimes/rarely* bored.
  3 are *often/always* good listeners.
  4 *don't often/don't usually* do lots of things at the same time.
  5 *sometimes/rarely* check their messages only once a day.
  6 *usually/hardly ever* have busy and stressful lives.
  7 *hardly ever/always* work at weekends.
  8 *sometimes/never* stop trying.

  b Number the adverbs of frequency in the box from 1 (most frequent) to 6 (least frequent). Use Exercise 4a to help you.

  | always *1* | hardly ever/rarely | never | often | sometimes | usually |

Meryl Streep

5 a Read the grammar box and choose the correct alternatives.

Adverbs of frequency

Use adverbs of frequency to talk about ¹*how often/ when* you do something.

Adverbs of frequency usually come ²*before/after* the verb *be*.

Successful people **are often** good listeners.

They usually come ³*before/after* other verbs.

... they **always look for** new and exciting experiences.

You can use *always, usually* and *often* with verbs in the negative. They come ⁴*before/after* the negative verb.

Successful people **don't often do** lots of things at the same time.

There are other expressions of frequency that you can use, e.g. *every day, once a week, all the time*. These usually come ⁵*at the end/in the middle* of a sentence.

They sometimes check their messages only **once a day**.

b 🔊 1.8 Listen to the sentences. What do you notice about the two letters in bold?
1 He doesn**'t o**ften try new things.
2 He sometimes asks **a l**ot **of** questions.
3 I**'m o**ften bored at weekends.
4 She goes to the cinema on**ce a** week.
5 You hardl**y e**ver **a**sk questions.

c Listen again and repeat.

6 a Complete the sentences with the adverbs in brackets.
1 Ben does one activity at a time. (always)
   Ben always does one activity at a time.
2 Ana tries a new activity. (once a month)
3 I'm successful in exams. (hardly ever)
4 We don't have a clear goal. (often)
5 I take time off in June. (sometimes)
6 Jon works hard. (all the time)
7 They're not busy in the morning. (usually)
8 I check my work emails at weekends. (rarely)

b Work in pairs. Take turns to ask and answer questions with *How often* and a phrase in the box.

be late	be really busy	eat pizza	get angry
go for a swim	go to the cinema
send something by post	sing in the shower

A: *How often are you late?*
B: *I'm hardly ever late. I always leave early for everything. How often do you go to the cinema?*

📱 Go to page 116 or your app for more information and practice.

Speaking

PREPARE

7 a 🔊 1.9 You're going to tell other students about a successful person. First, listen to Alex talking about a successful person he knows. Answer the questions.
1 Who is the person?
2 How old is she?
3 Why does Alex think she is successful?

b Listen again. How often does the person do these things?
1 get up early
2 go for a long walk
3 use public transport
4 look after her great-grandchildren

c Make notes about a successful person. It can be someone you know (e.g. a friend) or someone you don't know (e.g. someone famous). Think about:
- who the person is
- what they do
- why you think they are successful

SPEAK

8 Work in groups. Take turns to tell each other about your successful person. Ask people questions to get more information and use the Useful phrases to help you.

A: *My friend Dani often wins short film competitions.*
B: *That's great! What else does she do?*

Useful phrases
He/She sounds amazing/brilliant/fantastic!
Tell me/us more.
That's great!
What else does he/she do?

Develop your writing
page 87

1B | Successful people

9

1c A new lifestyle

- **Goal:** describe everyday activities
- **Grammar:** present simple and present continuous
- **Vocabulary:** everyday activities

Reading

1 a Marek and Kim are trying a new lifestyle. Look at the photos. What kind of things do you think they do?

b Read Marek's blog post and check your ideas.

Hi everyone! Kim and I are trying a new lifestyle. We usually live in the city, but this month we're living in a forest without electricity, internet, phones and things like that.

So, how am I writing this blog? Well, we come into town once a week to use the internet and buy some things we need. The town is about 10 km away and we always walk here – it's great exercise! I'm using the computer in the library at the moment, to check my email and to write to you. Kim's looking for some blankets in a shop because it's really cold at night!

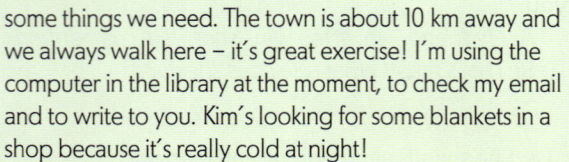

We're living in a really simple house which has a nice vegetable garden. Life is good, but it's hard work. We get up at 5.30 a.m. every day. We have a simple breakfast then work for most of the day. We pick vegetables in the garden and we collect wood in the forest. We finish work at about 6 p.m. In the evenings, we play cards, read or just sit in the garden … when the weather's nice. We go to bed early, too, usually around 9 p.m. We're not missing TV at all! Anyway, we're really enjoying it so far!

2 a Read Marek's post again and answer the questions.
1. How often do Marek and Kim go into town?
2. Where is Kim at the moment?
3. What time do they get up?
4. What do they do in the evenings?
5. What time do they go to bed?

b Work in pairs and discuss the questions.
1. Would you like to try this lifestyle?
2. Where would be a good place to do this in your country?
3. What do you think are the positive and negative things about this lifestyle?

Grammar

3 a Read the grammar box and choose the correct alternatives.

Present simple and present continuous

Use the present ¹*simple/continuous* to talk about facts, things which are generally true or something that happens regularly.
*The town **is** about 10 km away.*
*We usually **live** in the big city.*
*We **get up** at 5.30 a.m. every day.*

Use the present ²*simple/continuous* to describe something happening now.
***I'm using** the computer in the library.*

You can also use the present continuous to describe a ³*permanent/temporary* situation happening around now.
*Kim and I **are trying** a new lifestyle.*

It is common to use time expressions like *at the moment, right now* and *these days* with the present continuous.
***I'm using** the computer in the library **at the moment**.*

b Find and underline three more examples of the present simple and three of the present continuous in Marek's post in Exercise 1.

4 a 🔊 **1.10** We usually contract *be* in the present continuous. Listen and choose the alternative you hear.
  1 *We are/We're* having a great time.
  2 *She is/She's* eating a sandwich.
  3 *I am/I'm* working in the garden.
  4 *They are/They're* working outside.

 b 🔊 **1.11** Listen to the sentences with contractions and repeat.

5 Complete Marek's latest post with the correct forms of the verbs in brackets.

> Hi all! Sorry for not writing. Town is very far and we ¹_____ (not have) time to walk here every week. Anyway, only one week left! I ²_____ (sit) in the library, again. Things are the same here. Every day, we ³_____ (work) very hard from morning until night and we ⁴_____ (feel) tired all the time. To be honest, we ⁵_____ (want) to go home because we ⁶_____ (be) quite bored of this lifestyle. I ⁷_____ (think) about our TV and comfortable sofa right now!

6 a Complete the sentences so they are true for you.
  1 I'm … at the moment.
  2 I … every day.
  3 My family always …
  4 I'm … these days.
  5 I'm not … right now.

 b Work in pairs. Share your ideas and ask questions to find out more information.
  A: *I'm learning Chinese at the moment.*
  B: *Really? Is it difficult?*

📱 Go to page 116 or your app for more information and practice.

Vocabulary

7 a Complete phrases 1–8 with the words in the box. Use Marek's posts in Exercises 1 and 5 to help you.

| check | get | have | play | spend | start/finish |
| ~~take~~ | watch | | | | |

  1 *take* a break/a picture
  2 _____ cards/video games
  3 _____ TV/a film
  4 _____ a shower/lunch
  5 _____ work/school
  6 _____ up/dressed
  7 _____ your email/social media
  8 _____ time with friends/family

 b Add the words in the box to phrases 1–8.

| a good time | a language course | a show | ~~a taxi~~ |
| home | money | the answers | the piano |

  1 *take a break/a picture/a taxi*

 c Work in pairs. Student A: say a verb from the box in Exercise 7a. Student B: say a noun in Exercise 7a or 7b that goes with it.

📱 Go to page 136 or your app for more vocabulary and practice.

Speaking

PREPARE

8 a 🔊 **1.12** You're going to describe a change in lifestyle. First, listen to a conversation between Paul and Stephanie. Which change of lifestyle below is Stephanie trying?
  • trying a new diet
  • living in a different place/country
  • living with little money
  • living without technology
  • working at night

 b Listen again and answer the questions.
  1 What different things does she do these days? Does she miss anything?
  2 How does she feel about it?

9 Imagine you're making a change to your lifestyle. Choose one of the topics in Exercise 8a or use one of your own ideas. Answer the questions below and make notes.
  • What change are you making? How is it different to your usual lifestyle?
  • How do you feel about it? Do you miss anything?

SPEAK

10 Work in pairs. Take turns to describe your change in lifestyle. Use your notes in Exercise 9 and the Useful phrases to help you.

> **Useful phrases**
> How's it going?
> Guess what I'm doing (at the moment)?
> Wow, that sounds (amazing/brilliant/great).
> I'm trying (a new sport).
> I miss (chocolate).

Develop your reading — page 88

1C | A new lifestyle

1D English in action

> **Goal:** ask for and check information

1. **Look at the pictures and answer the questions.**
   1. What's happening in each picture?
   2. What kind of help does each person need?
   3. Have you ever been in any of these situations?

2. a **1.13** **Listen to three conversations. Match them to three of pictures A–D.**

   b **Listen again and answer the questions.**
   1. Where does the man in Conversation 1 want to go?
   2. Which bus does the girl in Conversation 2 need to take?
   3. Which exercise does the girl in Conversation 3 need do?

3. a **1.14** **Listen and tick (✓) the phrases you hear.**

   Useful phrases

   Asking for information
   What do I need to do?
   Can you help me?

   Giving information
   It's this one here.
   You need to (buy a ticket).

   Checking someone understands
   Did you get that?
   Is that clear?

   Checking details
   Which (one) is it?
   Can you repeat that, please?

   b **Listen again and repeat.**

4. **Complete the conversations. Use the Useful phrases to help you.**
   1. **A:** Excuse me, I'm looking for somewhere that sells paper. Can you _help_ me?
      B: Sure. You _____ to go to *Clips* on the High Street.
   2. **A:** Is _____ clear?
      B: No, sorry, can you _____ that, please?
      A: Sure. Take the 9.52 train.
   3. **A:** Sorry, I missed that. What _____ I need to do?
      B: Read the paragraph, then answer the questions.
      A: Which paragraph is it?
      B: _____ this one here.

Speaking

> **PREPARE**

5. **Work in pairs. Practise the conversation below.**
   A: Hi. Can you help me? I'm not sure how to get to the transport museum.
   B: You need to take the 59 bus to Springfield Park, then change to the 342. Is that clear?
   A: I think so. I need to take the number 59, then the 342.
   B: Yes, that's right.
   A: Thanks again.

> **SPEAK**

6. **Student A go to page 151 and Student B go to page 153.**

Go online for the Roadmap video.

Check and reflect

1 Complete each question with one word.

1 What time ~~do~~ you get up in the morning?
2 What ___ your favourite food?
3 Whose pen ___ this?
4 ___ Long is the lesson?
5 Which film do ___ want to watch?
6 How ___ brothers and sisters have you got?

2 a Look at the topics below. Write a question for each one to ask another student. Use a different question word each time.
- music/films/TV
- family/friends
- free time
- birthday
- work/studies
- food/drink

b Work in pairs and ask each other the questions you wrote. Ask some follow-up questions.

3 a Choose the correct alternatives.

1 *What/Who*'s your favourite actor?
2 *How long/How many* does it take you to get ready in the morning?
3 *Whose/Who's* birthday do you always remember?
4 *How long/How many* hours of TV do you watch every day?
5 *How/What* do you like to relax in the evening?

b Work in pairs. Ask and answer the questions.

4 a Complete the sentences with one of the adverbs in the box so that they are true for you. You can use them more than once.

> always   hardly ever   never   often   rarely
> sometimes   usually

1 I get up early at the weekend.
2 I listen carefully to other people.
3 I arrive late to class.
4 I plan my time well.
5 My teacher gives me homework.
6 I'm happy when I wake up in the morning.
7 I work/study at the weekend.
8 My friends are busy at the weekend.

b Work in groups. Compare your sentences. Are any of them similar?

5 a Match verbs 1–8 with endings a–h.

1	have	a	care of yourself
2	take	b	your time well
3	take	c	new things
4	listen	d	clear goals
5	start	e	again
6	ask	f	a lot of questions
7	try	g	carefully
8	plan	h	time off

b Choose five of the phrases and write sentences about you for each one.

6 Choose the correct alternatives.

A: Hi Janice, what ¹*do you do/are you doing* at the moment?
B: Nothing really, I ²*just watch/'m just watching* TV.
A: Can I ask you a favour? I ³*have/'m having* my dance class tonight but my babysitter just cancelled. Can you help?
B: Sure! I ⁴*don't do/'m not doing* anything important right now.
A: That's great! Kieran ⁵*does/is doing* his homework at the moment, but then he ⁶*usually plays/'s usually playing* video games for an hour before bed. I should be back by then. Thanks a lot!
B: No problem!

7 a Complete the questions with the correct form of the words in brackets.

1 What time ___ (you / usually go) to bed?
2 What ___ (you / study) in English class this week?
3 What ___ (you / do) right now?
4 How often ___ (you / listen) to podcasts?
5 What ___ (you / wear) today?

b Work in pairs. Ask and answer the questions.

8 a Complete the everyday activities with a verb.

1 I always ___ my email first thing in the morning.
2 I ___ work/school at 9 a.m.
3 I ___ time with my friends every weekend.
4 I never ___ up early at the weekend.
5 I ___ video games in my free time.
6 I don't always ___ breakfast.
7 I try to ___ a break every hour when I'm studying.
8 I ___ TV every evening.

b Which of the sentences are true for you? Change the others so they are true.

c Work in pairs. Compare your sentences. Ask some follow-up questions to find out more information.

Reflect

How confident do you feel about the statements below? Write 1–5 (1 = not very confident, 5 = very confident).
- I can get to know someone.
- I can describe habits and routines.
- I can describe typical everyday activities.
- I can ask for and check information.

Want more practice?
Go to your Workbook or app.

2A One of those days

> **Goal:** describe a memorable day
> **Grammar:** past simple
> **Vocabulary:** feelings

Vocabulary and listening

1 Look at the photos. Do you think the people in the photos are having a good or a bad day? Why/Why not?

2 a Which adjectives in the box can you use to describe the people in the photos? More than one answer may be possible for each photo.

afraid angry bored excited happy nervous relaxed stressed surprised worried

b Choose the correct alternatives.
1 Sadie is *angry/nervous* about her big presentation – there are 600 people in the room.
2 Hamza is quite *relaxed/worried* about his interview. He's not nervous.
3 I'm so *bored/stressed* here. There's nothing to do except watch TV.
4 Pablo is so *surprised/excited* about his holiday – he talks about it all the time.
5 She's very *stressed/afraid* at the moment. I think she's having a very difficult time at work.
6 Matteo is *nervous/afraid* because he has an exam tomorrow.

3 a How would you feel in these situations? Think of as many adjectives as possible for each one.
1 You find out that someone at work is saying bad things about you to your colleagues.
2 You're lying on your sofa at the end of a long day, watching a film.
3 You have a job interview tomorrow morning.
4 You're lost in a big city at night.
5 You're graduating from university.
6 You're having a fun day with your friends.
7 You receive a present in the post from someone you don't know.
8 You have to pay a bill but you don't have any money.

b Work in pairs and compare your answers.

4 a Choose three of the adjectives in Exercise 2a. For each one, write a sentence describing a situation when you feel this way.

When I feel like this I talk a lot, I walk around the room and I can't relax. (nervous)

b Work in pairs and read your sentences to your partner. Guess which adjective your partner is describing.

Go to page 137 or your app for more vocabulary and practice.

5 a 2.1 Listen to Lynn talking about her job interview. Tick (✓) how she felt that day.

angry bored happy nervous relaxed stressed surprised

b Listen again and decide if the sentences are true (T) or false (F).
1 Lynn woke up late because her alarm didn't go off.
2 She had a big breakfast.
3 She went to her job interview by bus.
4 She used her computer in the presentation.
5 The interview went well.

Grammar

6 Read the grammar box and choose the correct alternatives.

Past simple

Use the past simple to talk about ¹*finished/unfinished* actions or states in the past.
I **took** the bus to the interview.
I **was** angry.
Use *was/wasn't* and *were/weren't* to make the past simple of ²*be/have*.
The interviewers **weren't** happy.
Regular past simple verbs end in ³*-ed/-ing*.
It **started** badly.
Some verbs are irregular.
I **woke** up late.
I **got** into my car.

7 a 🔊 **2.2** Listen to the pronunciation of the past simple verbs in the box and complete the table.

arrived	decided	deleted	ended	played
looked	showed	stopped	talked	tried
wanted	watched			

/d/	/ɪd/	/t/
showed	decided	looked

b Listen again and repeat.

8 a Complete the text with the past simple form of the verbs in brackets.

Several years ago, I ¹_____ (go) to a dinner party at a colleague's house. When I ²_____ (arrive), he took my coat and umbrella, and ³_____ (show) me to my seat at the table. Looking around, I realised that I was the only person from work. Even worse, his friends all ⁴_____ (know) each other really well – I ⁵_____ (try) to join in the conversations, but it ⁶_____ (be) hard. However, I ⁷_____ (notice) a woman at the other end of the table. I ⁸_____ (think) she was beautiful, and I really ⁹_____ (want) to talk to her, but she was too far away. Anyway, I was bored after dinner so I ¹⁰_____ (decide) to leave early. I put on my coat, picked up my umbrella, and ¹¹_____ (walk) to the bus stop. But when I opened the umbrella, I saw it wasn't mine. Just then, I ¹²_____ (hear) a voice behind me say, 'I think you've got my umbrella.' I looked round, and it was the beautiful woman from the dinner party. That was ten years ago, and now we're happily married!

b Work in pairs. Talk about a time when you felt:
- nervous
- bored
- excited
- surprised

📱 Go to page 118 or your app for more information and practice.

Speaking

PREPARE

9 You're going to describe a memorable day. Choose a day you want to describe and think about:
1 Was it a good or bad day?
2 What happened at the start of the day?
3 What were the main events?
4 How did you feel during the day?
5 What happened in the end?

SPEAK

10 Work in groups. Describe your day to your group. Use the Useful phrases to help you. Are any of your days similar?

Useful phrases

It started well/badly.
First of all, (I woke up late).
Then, (I missed my bus).
After that, (I got lost).
Finally, (I went home).

Develop your reading
page 89

2A | One of those days

15

2B You're never too old

› **Goal:** ask about and describe past events
› **Grammar:** past simple negative and questions
› **Vocabulary:** past time expressions

YOU DON'T HAVE TO BE YOUNG TO DO AMAZING THINGS

This week we're looking at three people who did something amazing later in their lives. Who were they? What did they do? Why did they do it?

1 Kimani Maruge
Kimani Maruge was born in Kenya. When he was a child, people in his country had to pay to go to school, so he didn't learn to read and write. Then, in 2003, primary schools became free so he decided to get an education. He started school for the first time at 84 years old. Learning wasn't easy for him but he worked hard. This experience completely changed his life. In fact, in 2005, he travelled to New York to talk to people at the United Nations about free education.

2 Harriette Thompson
Harriette Thompson was born in 1923 in the US. She worked as a piano player for most of her life. On 23rd May 1999, one of Harriette's friends decided to walk the San Diego marathon for charity. Harriette joined her but she didn't walk – she ran. She was 76 years old. She ran the marathon every year between 1999 and 2015, except for one year when she was very ill. When she was 94 years old, she became the oldest woman to complete a marathon. It took her 7 hours, 24 minutes and 36 seconds and she collected more than $100,000 for charity.

3 Laila Denmark
Laila Denmark was born in 1898 in Atlanta, USA. She wanted to become a doctor so she could help children. Studying medicine wasn't usual for women at the time. In fact, she was the only woman in a class of 52 students. Most people stop working when they're about 65, but Dr Denmark didn't retire until she was 103 years old! She lived for 11 more years.

Reading and vocabulary

1 Look at the photos. What amazing thing do you think you each person did?

2 a Read the article. Match descriptions 1–3 to photos A–C and answer the questions in the introduction.

b Read the article again and answer the questions.
  1 When did Kimani Maruge start school?
  2 When did he travel to the US?
  3 When did Harriette first run a marathon?
  4 When did she become the oldest woman to run a marathon?
  5 When did Laila Denmark retire?
  6 How old was she when she died?

c Work in pairs. Who do you think did the most amazing thing? Why?

3 a Put the time expressions in order from the most recent (1) to the oldest (6).

> in 2018   last month *1*   on 23rd May 2017
> six weeks ago   until 2015   when I was five

b Complete the expressions with the words in the box.

> ago   in   last   on   until   when

  1 _____ I was a child   4 _____ my 10th birthday
  2 _____ week   5 _____ last year
  3 A few years _____   6 _____ 2015

c Write six sentences using each expression.
  When I was a child, I loved playing outside.

d Work in pairs. Tell each other your sentences. Give more information.
  When I was a child, I loved playing outside. I always played football in the park with my brother.

📱 Go to your app for more practice.

Grammar

4 Read the grammar box and choose the correct alternatives.

Past simple negative and questions

Use ¹*didn't/doesn't* + infinitive to make past simple negative sentences.
She **didn't walk** – she ran.
Dr Denmark **didn't retire** until 2001.
Use ²*isn't and aren't/wasn't and weren't* with the verb *be*.
Schools **weren't** free.
Learning **wasn't** easy for him.
Use ³*do/did* + infinitive to make past simple questions.
What **did** they do?
Why **did** they do it?
Use ⁴*did/was and were* in past simple questions with *be*.
Who **were** they?

5 a 🔊 2.3 Listen to the conversations. Notice the pronunciation of *did/didn't* and *was/wasn't*.

1   **A:** Did you learn to sing at school?
    B: Yes, I did.
2   **A:** Did she finish the marathon?
    B: No, she didn't.
3   **A:** How old were you?
    B: I wasn't very old, actually.
4   **A:** Was he from Italy?
    B: No, he wasn't.

b Work in pairs. Listen again and repeat.

6 a Use the prompts to make questions with *did, was* or *were*.

1   How / you / learn to play the piano?
    How did you learn to play the piano?
2   it / difficult to get into your university?
3   When / you / get your driving licence?
4   you / happy with your exam results?
5   you / enjoy water skiing?
6   he / win the race?

b Complete each answer with *didn't, wasn't* or *weren't*.

a   When I was 35. I _____ have lessons until I was in my 30s.
b   It was really hard. Maths _____ an easy exam.
c   I taught myself. I _____ have a teacher.
d   No, we _____ .
e   I loved it. It _____ scary at all.
f   No, he _____ . He came second.

c Work in pairs. Take it in turns to ask a question in Exercise 6a and answer with a response from 6b.

📱 Go to page 118 or your app for more information and practice.

Speaking

PREPARE

7 a 🔊 2.4 You're going to talk about something special you did in the past. First, listen to Dan and Megan. What did Megan do?

b Write three questions Dan could ask Megan to find out more information.

c 🔊 2.5 Listen to the rest of their conversation. Did Dan ask any of your questions? What other things did you learn about Megan?

8 Think of something special that you did in the past, for example: an event, learning something new or doing something for the first time. Answer the questions below.
- What did you do?
- When did you do it?
- Where did you do it?
- Who did you do it with?
- Why did you do it?

SPEAK

9 a Work in pairs. Tell each other about what you did. Ask each other questions to find out as much information as possible.

b Work in different pairs. Tell each other what you learnt about your first partner.

Develop your writing
page 90

17

2c Unusual tastes

> **Goal:** describe a special dish
> **Grammar:** quantifiers
> **Vocabulary:** adjectives to describe food

Listening & vocabulary

1 **Write down as many types of food as possible for the categories below.**
- meat and fish
- fruit
- vegetables

2 a **Look at the photos and discuss the questions.**
  1 Do you know any of the dishes?
  2 What ingredients do you think are in each dish?
  3 Which country do you think each one is from?
  4 Which would you like to try? Why?

  b **Read descriptions 1–5 and match them to photos A–E. Do you think they sound nice?**

  1 ***Ahi Poke*** Hawaii
  This popular fish salad from Hawaii is made with tuna, onions, garlic, seeds, soy sauce and oil. People usually eat it as a starter, or as a side dish with their lunch.

  2 ***Brigadeiro*** Brazil
  This is a traditional dessert but sometimes, people just eat it as a snack. It's made from milk, butter and chocolate. People usually eat *brigadeiros* at parties, and they're delicious!

  3 ***Stargazy pie*** UK
  This is a fish pie made with the fish heads on the outside, like they are looking (or 'gazing') at the stars. Its other main ingredients are potatoes, eggs, butter and onions.

  4 ***Po'e*** Tahiti
  This is a popular dessert in Tahiti, but people sometimes eat it as a side dish, too. It is a sweet dish made with bananas or mangoes, some sugar and some coconut cream.

  5 ***Nasi Lemak*** Malaysia
  Some people describe this as the national dish of Malaysia. People usually eat it for breakfast, but you can also eat it at any time during the day. It includes rice, egg and cucumber, and often comes with a hot sauce called *sambal*.

3 🔊 2.6 **Listen to three people talking about some of the dishes in Exercise 2. Which dish does each person try? Do they like it?**

4 a **Listen to the conversations again. In which conversation (1, 2 or 3) do you hear the adjectives in the box?**

   delicious   dry   creamy   fresh   hot   light
   plain   sour   sweet *1*

  b **Which adjectives do you think are positive and which are negative?**

  c **Work in pairs. Think of two dishes or types of food for each adjective.**

  📱 Go to page 137 or your app for more vocabulary and practice.

Grammar

5 🔊 **2.7** Listen to the extracts and choose the correct alternatives.
1. Actually, there isn't *any/a* sugar in it.
2. But there's a *few/lot of* chocolate and milk.
3. Have *some/any* sauce with it.
4. It's got *a few/lots of* chilli in it.
5. It's *a/an* salad from my part of the world.
6. Yes, it has a *few/little* oil in it.
7. Yes, there are a *few/little* herbs and spices to give it more flavour.
8. I usually have *no/a bit of* bread with it, too.

6 Read the grammar box and choose the correct alternatives.

Quantifiers

Use *a/an* to introduce ¹*singular countable/ uncountable* nouns.
There's **a whole onion** in this dish.
Use *any, some, a lot of/lots of* with both countable and uncountable nouns.
There **are some herbs** and spices in the soup.
Put **lots of pepper** in the soup, but please don't add **any salt** to it.
Use *a few* with ²*plural countable/uncountable* nouns.
This recipe needs **a few eggs** – not many, just two or three.
Use *a little/a bit of* with ³*singular countable/ uncountable* nouns.
There's just **a little sugar** in it – not too much.
Any, a few and *a little* describe a ⁴*large/small* amount.
A lot of/lots of describes a ⁵*big/small* amount.
Just **a little milk** for me, please - not too much.
Wow! There's **a lot of** chilli in this sauce!

7 a 🔊 **2.8** Listen to the sentences. What do you notice about the letters in bold?
1. The**re's a** lot of salt in this.
2. The**re a**re some eggs in the fridge.
3. The**re i**sn't any sugar in it.
4. The**re's a** bit of soy sauce.
5. The**re are a** few apples on the table.

b Listen again and repeat.

8 Complete the description with the words in the box.

| a lot of | any (x2) | few | little | lots |

Although there are ¹_____ different types of white pizza, there aren't ²_____ that are like the one from Pennsylvania, USA. Although it's called a pizza, it's more like a pie. There isn't ³_____ meat on it, but there's ⁴_____ of cheese. It's usually made using a ⁵_____ different types of cheese, and a ⁶_____ olive oil is poured on top before baking. These ingredients give it a great flavour.

9 a Complete the sentences so they are true for you.
1. I eat a lot of …
2. I like some types of …
3. There's a/some … in my favourite dish.
4. I try to eat a little/a few … every day.
5. There isn't/aren't any … in my fridge at home at the moment.
6. I don't like any kinds of …

b Work in pairs and compare your answers. Do you have anything in common?

📱 Go to page 118 or your app for more information and practice.

Speaking

PREPARE

10 You're going to describe a dish. First, choose one of the ideas below and make notes. Use the adjectives in Exercise 4a and the Useful phrases to help you.
- an unusual dish that you know
- a dish you really liked when you were a child
- a dish you know how to make
- your favourite dish

Useful phrases
It's made from (eggs/chocolate/cheese).
It's got some/a little/lots of/a few (sugar/ chocolate/herbs) in it.
It looks (dry).
It tastes (delicious).
People usually eat it (on New Year's Eve).

SPEAK

11 a Work in groups. Describe your dish to your group. Listen to other students describe their dishes and ask questions.
A: *This dish has lots of herbs and spices in it.*
B: *Is it hot?*

b Which dish would you most like to try?

Develop your listening page 91

2C | Unusual tastes

19

2D English in action

Goal: show interest and excitement

1 Look at the photos. What are the people doing? How are they feeling?

2 a 🔊 2.14 Listen to four conversations and answer the questions.
   1 Why is Ali happy?
   2 How did Marco help Fran?
   3 What time is Ricky's party?
   4 What did Simone win?

b Choose the correct alternatives to complete the extracts from the conversations.
   1 80 percent? *That's/ What's* brilliant!
   2 *It's/ They're* lovely. Thanks!
   3 That *looks/ sounds* great!
   4 I love your curries. They're *really/ so* good.
   5 No way! That's *amazing!/ great!*

c Listen to the conversations again and check your answers.

3 a 🔊 2.15 Listen to the sentences. Does speaker 1 or speaker 2 show interest/excitement in each one?
   1 That sounds fantastic!
   2 Amazing!
   3 How exciting!
   4 What a great idea!
   5 That sounds really interesting!

b 🔊 2.16 Listen to the speakers showing interest/ excitement again and repeat.

4 a Complete the conversations with an appropriate response. Use the Useful phrases to help you. More than one answer might be possible.
   1 **A:** I'm going to run a marathon next month.
      B: Really? That _____ exciting! And difficult!
   2 **A:** We were in Mexico this time last week.
      B: _____ ! _____ you have a good time?
   3 **A:** I've just got my dream job!
      B: Really? That's _____ !
   4 **A:** I'm making your favourite pasta for dinner.
      B: _____ !
   5 **A:** We went to that new Italian restaurant last night.
      B: Really? What _____ you think of it?
      A: It was _____ !

Useful phrases

Creating interest
Guess what (happened to me)!?
Guess what I did/where I went?

Responding to information
Great!/Brilliant!/Fantastic!/Amazing!
It's/They're (delicious/lovely).
That's (amazing/great).
How (exciting/amazing/fantastic)!
What a (good idea).
That sounds (lovely/wonderful)!
No way!

Asking follow-up questions
What happened (next/after that)?
How did that/it go?
Who did you go with?

b Work in pairs. Practise the conversations with the appropriate intonation.

Speaking

PREPARE

5 a Work in pairs. You're going to share some exciting news. It can be real or imagined. Student A go to page 151 and Student B go to page 152.

SPEAK

b Share your news with each other. Show interest and excitement when appropriate. Use the Useful phrases to help you.

Go online for the Roadmap video.

Check and reflect

1 a Complete the sentences with the correct form of the verbs in the box.

be   get up   go   have   meet   play   take watch

1. I _____ a really good film last month.
2. My family and I _____ on holiday last summer.
3. I _____ a great meal last night.
4. My sister _____ a train to Moscow two weeks ago.
5. I _____ some video games last night.
6. My friend and I _____ at a coffee shop last week.
7. I _____ late yesterday, after 10 a.m.
8. I _____ bored yesterday.

b Work in pairs. Which sentences are true for you? Give more information about them.

2 a Complete each sentence with an adjective of feeling. The first and last letter of each word are given.
1. I've got so much work to do. I'm really s____d.
2. Our holiday starts tomorrow. I'm so e____d!
3. I'm a____d of spiders. I hate them.
4. Jon never gets stressed. He's always r____d.
5. When Sam dropped Abi's phone, she got really a____y with him.
6. I've got my driving test tomorrow and I'm really n____s.
7. Billy just won a competition. He's really h____y.
8. Everyone was s____d when they heard the news.

b Work in pairs. Choose five of the adjectives and talk about when you last felt like that.
I was angry last week when I lost my keys.

3 a Make each sentence negative.
1. We went to the gym last night.
2. Sara was happy yesterday.
3. I went to bed late last night.
4. They were very busy last week.
5. We played cards yesterday.
6. Jimmy lived in San Diego when he was a child.

b Work in pairs. Tell each other three things you wanted to do yesterday but didn't do.
I wanted to go to the gym but I didn't have time.

4 a Put the words in the correct order to make questions.
1. last night / you / did / do / what / ?
2. you / who / chat to / yesterday / did / ?
3. were / last weekend / you / where / ?
4. did / go / what time / last night / to bed / you / ?
5. have for dinner / what / yesterday / you / did / ?
6. was / your / what colour / first car / ?
7. TV / last / you / did / night / watch / ?
8. this English course / decide / why / you / did / do / to / ?

b Work in pairs. Take turns to ask and answer the questions.

5 a Match the sentence halves.
1. I didn't learn to swim until I was
2. Cara was born on
3. We first met each other last
4. Liam started a new job a few weeks
5. I moved to Rome in
6. I didn't study English when

a. year.
b. 17th April 1999.
c. ten years old.
d. I was at school.
e. ago.
f. 2017.

b Work in pairs. Tell each other some things you did in the past using some past time expressions.
I went to France last week.

6 a Choose the correct alternatives.

This is a meal that I cook for friends. It's simple but delicious and they love it!

I make pasta with a tomato sauce. I cook ¹*some/a few* spaghetti and then I fry half ²*an/some* onion in ³*a little/a few* oil. Then I add ⁴*a few/any* herbs and ⁵*a few/a little* garlic but not too much. Finally, I mix the spaghetti and sauce together. I then put ⁶*a lot/a lot of* parmesan cheese on top because I love it so much. There isn't ⁷*any/a little* meat in this dish because I'm vegetarian but you can put ⁸*an/some* in if you like.

b Work in pairs. Describe your favourite meal. What is it? What's in it?

7 a Put the letters in italics in the correct order to make adjectives.
1. This orange juice is really *etswe*.
2. This sandwich doesn't taste of anything. It's very *ialpn*.
3. I love this chocolate cake. It's *coleusidi*.
4. Let's eat something *thigl* like a salad.
5. Aargh! This lemon juice is really *orus*!
6. Is this milk *shref* or old?
7. I can't eat this cake. It's too *meaycr*.

b Work in pairs. Think of other food that you can describe with each adjective in Exercise 7a.

c Tell each other three foods you think are delicious and three foods you think are plain. Do you agree?

Reflect

How confident do you feel about the statements below? Write 1–5 (1 = not very confident, 5 = very confident).
- I can describe a memorable day.
- I can ask about and describe past events.
- I can describe a special dish.
- I can show interest and excitement.

Want more practice?
Go to your Workbook or app.

3A Urban escapes

- **Goal:** compare places to visit
- **Grammar:** comparatives
- **Vocabulary:** adjectives to describe places

Vocabulary and reading

1 Look at the pairs of photos A–C and discuss the questions.
  1. Do you know any of the places in the photos?
  2. Which place would you most like to visit? Why?

2 a Do you think the adjectives in the box are positive (P) or negative (N)?

> beautiful P   cheap   clean   crowded   dirty
> exciting   interesting   lively   modern   noisy
> old   peaceful   popular

b Work in pairs and compare your answers. Do you agree?

3 a Complete each sentence with an adjective in Exercise 2a.
  1. This area has become very _____. Everybody likes to come here.
  2. Look at that view, it's really _____!
  3. I love this city, but the air is so _____.
  4. Don't visit the museum on a Saturday, it gets very _____.
  5. There's a nice mix of both _____ and old buildings by the river.

b Work in pairs and discuss the questions.
  1. Which of the adjectives could you use to describe the places in Exercise 1?
  2. Which of the adjectives could you use to describe where you live?

4 a Read the travel forum posts and decide which photos in Exercise 1 the people are discussing.

1

Simone
Hey! I'm in London for the weekend. Where are the best places to eat out?

Elisabeth
Camden Market! There are lots of choices, with food from all over the world, and it's quite cheap. It's a really lively area, with lots of exciting things to do. It's an interesting area, too – there's a mix of old and modern buildings.

Rebecca
Camden Market is great, but it can get very crowded. I'd recommend St Katharine's Docks, a bit further away. It's a lovely little area where you can relax and have a nice meal, and it's not as noisy as Camden Market. I think it's cheaper and quieter, too!

2

Barry
Hi everyone, my wife and I are going to Rio de Janeiro next month. Can you recommend which beaches to go to?

Pedro
Well, I just love Copacabana. It's longer than the other beaches in the city, so there's lots of space to play volleyball or just relax. It's livelier than other beaches, too – you can have lots of fun there!

Patrizio
I'd recommend Grumari or Prainha – these two beaches are a few kilometres out of Rio. They're cleaner than the city beaches, too, which are noisier and more crowded.

Bethany
I agree with Pedro. You should definitely visit Copacabana and other beaches in the city, but Prainha and Grumari are better. They're less noisy and more beautiful, in my opinion.

b **Read the forum posts again and decide if the sentences are true (T) or false (F).**
1 Camden Market is a peaceful place.
2 Camden Market is a popular place.
3 St. Katharine's Docks is near Camden Market.
4 Copacabana beach is busy.
5 Grumari and Prainha are outside the city.

c **Work in pairs. Are there any similar places in your country?**

Go to page 138 or your app for more vocabulary and practice.

Grammar

5 a **Read the grammar box and choose the correct alternatives.**

Comparatives

Use *be* + comparative adjective + *than* to compare two things.
*The market **is more popular than** the park.*
To make comparatives, add *-er* or *-ier* to **¹short/long** adjectives.
*The castle is **older** than the bridge.*
*This exercise is **easier** than the last one.*
Use *more* or *less* before **²short/long** adjectives.
*South Beach is **more beautiful** than North Beach.*
*Campbell's restaurant is **less popular** than Gino's.*
Some adjectives are **³regular/irregular**, e.g. *good – better*.
*Woodland Park is **better** than the riverside.*
You can use *(not) as* + adjective + *as* to say two things are or aren't the same.
*This restaurant is **as good as** the one we went to yesterday.*
*This shop **isn't as cheap as** the supermarket, but I like it.*

b **Find and underline one example of each comparative form in the forum posts.**

6 a 🔊 **3.1 Listen to the sentences and notice how the weak forms of *-er* and *than* are pronounced.**
1 The streets are dirtier than they were five years ago.
2 The north of the city is older than the south of the city.
3 This part of the beach is cleaner than the other part.
4 My town is busier than yours.

b **Listen again and repeat the sentences.**

7 **Complete the description with the correct form of the adjectives in brackets.**

One of my favourite places to escape to in Munich is the Viktualienmarkt, a fresh food market in the centre of the city. It's ¹_____ (quiet) than the area around it and some products are ²_____ (cheap) as those in the supermarket – sometimes cheaper!
But when I really want to escape the city, I go to the English Garden. It's ³_____ (peaceful) than the Viktualienmarkt, and the air is ⁴_____ (not dirty) as the rest of the city. You can always find a quiet place to relax because it's so big. In fact, it's ⁵_____ (big) than Central Park in New York!

8 a **Compare the places using the adjectives in Exercise 2a.**
1 Rio de Janeiro / Madrid
  I think Rio de Janeiro is more beautiful than Madrid.
2 my town or city / Paris
3 the desert / the mountains
4 the parks in my town or city / the countryside
5 the cities in my country / the cities in the US

b **Work in pairs and compare your ideas.**

Go to page 120 or your app for more information and practice.

Speaking

PREPARE

9 a 🔊 **3.2 You're going to make a list of top ten places to visit. First, listen to Mark and Sandra talking about an article they have to write. Which two places do they choose to write about?**

b **Listen again and answer the questions.**
1 Why doesn't Sandra like Mark's first choices?
2 Why does Mark like the Louvre?
3 What does Sandra say about the British Museum?

10 a **Make your own list. Write two places for each of the categories below. They can be places in your own country or other countries.**
- famous buildings
- beaches
- street markets
- parks
- places to eat
- shopping areas

b **Write some adjectives next to each place.**

SPEAK

11 a **Work in pairs. Compare your lists using the adjectives you wrote and agree on two places for each category.**
  A: *Bondi Beach is really beautiful, but I think South Bay is more beautiful and more peaceful*
  B: *OK, let's choose South Bay*

b **Share your list with the rest of the class. Did anyone else make the same choices as you?**

Develop your reading
page 92

3A | Urban escapes

23

3B A place to stay

> **Goal:** choose a place to stay
> **Grammar:** superlatives
> **Vocabulary:** hotels and places to stay

Vocabulary and reading

1 Work in groups and discuss the questions.
   1 Do you like staying in hotels? Why/Why not?
   2 What are the most important things for you when you choose a hotel?

2 a Work in pairs. Match words 1–10 with a–j.

1 airport	a room
2 breakfast	b service
3 organised	c star
4 free	d out
5 room	e included
6 double	f reception
7 sea	g transfer
8 four-	h tour
9 24-hour	i view
10 check	j parking

b Complete the sentences with one of the phrases.
   1 We don't need to take a taxi. The hotel provides a free _____ .
   2 Is there a late _____ ? I don't want to get up yet!
   3 Here are your keys. There's _____ in the price, but not lunch and dinner.
   4 Excuse me. We asked for a _____ , but we can only see the car park from our window.
   5 Let's order some _____ – I'm hungry!
   6 Is there a _____ ? We're going to arrive in the middle of the night.
   7 We'd like to visit the city tomorrow. Can you recommend an _____ ?
   8 We have a _____ for the same price as a single – would you like to book it?

3 a Think about the last time you stayed in a hotel and make notes. Use the phrases in Exercise 2a.

b Work in pairs. Tell each other about your hotels. Ask questions to find out more information.
   A: I stayed in a modern five-star hotel for work.
   B: Was it nice?
   A: Not really, it was too big.

📱 Go to page 138 or your app for more vocabulary and practice.

4 a Look at the photos in the magazine article. What do you think you can do in each place?

b Read the article and check your ideas.

We asked you to share your interesting hotel experiences with us from around the world. Here are our top choices.

BELA VISTA HOSTEL Peru
Shaun Tyson

We had a great time at the Bela Vista. It had some of the best views of anywhere we stayed in South America – we booked the room at the top of the hostel because you can see the furthest from it. Also, it's the biggest room. We spent an hour or two there every day, relaxing with a cold drink and enjoying the view. We loved their organised tours of the forest – they were amazing! But the best thing is, it's the least expensive place to stay in the area (with breakfast included every day!).

MATAHARI VILLAGE Indonesia
Juliette Wilson

Last year we travelled through South-East Asia and stayed in lots of modern hotels. So, when we came to Matahari Village, it was a really nice change. Actually, it was the nicest place we stayed in. We learnt about local cooking in the day, met people from the area, and at night we stayed in beautiful wooden houses. The beds inside didn't look very comfortable, but in fact it was the most comfortable place we stayed in all holiday!

THE PRINCESS MARGARITA RESORT Seychelles
Tristan Norris

This summer, my wife and I wanted to do something a bit special. We stayed in the 'Water Room' at The Princess Margarita Resort. The room is actually in the sea and you can see tropical fish through the glass floor. It's the most beautiful view ever. So if you're looking for a peaceful place to stay, then I definitely recommend it. Fish are the quietest neighbours in the world! At the end of our holiday, we didn't want to check out.

5 a Read the article again and match the descriptions to the places.
1 It's cheaper than other local places.
  Bela Vista Hostel
2 You can learn something new there.
3 There isn't any noise.
4 You have a view under your feet.
5 You can see a long way from one of the rooms.
6 It's a traditional experience.

b Work in pairs and discuss the questions.
1 Which of these places would/wouldn't you like to stay in? Why? Why not?
2 Are there any places like this in your country?

Grammar

6 a Read the grammar box and choose the correct alternatives.

Superlatives

Use *the* + superlative adjective to compare.
*Hostels are **the cheapest** places to stay in the city.*
To make superlative adjectives, add *-est* or *-iest* to [1] *short/long* adjectives.
*It's the **biggest** hotel in the area.*
*He's the **funniest** person I know.*
Use *the most* or *the least* before [2] *short/long* adjectives.
*TenX is **the most modern** hotel in the city.*
*It was **the least comfortable** room in the hotel.*
Some adjectives are irregular, e.g. *bad - worse - worst.*
*It's **the worst** hotel in the city.*

b Find and underline eight superlatives in the article.

7 a 3.3 Listen to the sentences and notice how the superlatives are pronounced.
1 It's the easiest place to find.
2 It's the oldest building in the area.
3 This is the ugliest hotel in town.
4 They have the nicest food.

b Listen again and repeat.

8 Complete each sentence with the superlative form of the adjective in brackets.
1 This is ___ (small) room in the hotel, but it's very quiet.
2 The New Hotel is ___ (modern) hotel in the area. It was built last year.
3 Where's ___ (good) place to stay in this town? I've never been here before.
4 The hotels here are quite cheap, but the hostel next door is ___ (expensive) option – it's only £15 a night!
5 This is ___ (pretty) part of town.
6 There are the ___ (amazing) views from the roof. I took lots of photos!

9 a Complete the questions about the places in the article with the superlative form of the adjective in brackets.
Which place do you think …
1 is ___ (expensive)?
2 is ___ (cheap)?
3 has ___ (good) restaurant?
4 has ___ (nice) rooms?
5 is ___ (easy) to get to?
6 is ___ (difficult) to get to?
7 has ___ (interesting) organised tours?
8 is ___ (far) from your country?

b Work in pairs and ask and answer the questions. Do you agree with each other?

Go to page 120 or your app for more information and practice.

Speaking

PREPARE

10 3.4 You're going to plan a trip. First, listen to Pat, Andrea and Shannon discussing three places to stay: Casa Tranquila, The Happy Campers Village and The Mantra Resort. Answer the questions.
1 Which hotel is the most expensive?
2 Which hotel is the cheapest?
3 Where do they decide to go?

11 a Imagine you're planning a class trip to New York and you need to decide where to stay. First, decide how important these things are for you (1 = not important and 5 = very important).
• close to the centre • modern
• noise • size of the room
• cost • facilities (wifi, parking, etc.)

b Go to page 152. Read the information about three hotels and choose where you want to stay.

SPEAK

12 Work in groups. Explain your choice with the other students in your group and try to agree on a place to stay. Use the Useful phrases to help you.
A: *I think we should stay at the Homestyle because it's close to the centre and it's the cheapest.*
B: *I'm not sure. I'd like somewhere quiet and it's the noisiest!*

Useful phrases
I think we should stay at (the Miramar) because it (has the best views).
Why don't we (stay in this hotel)?
That one is too (expensive/noisy).
This one is (nearer) than (that one).

Develop your writing page 93

3c Never ever

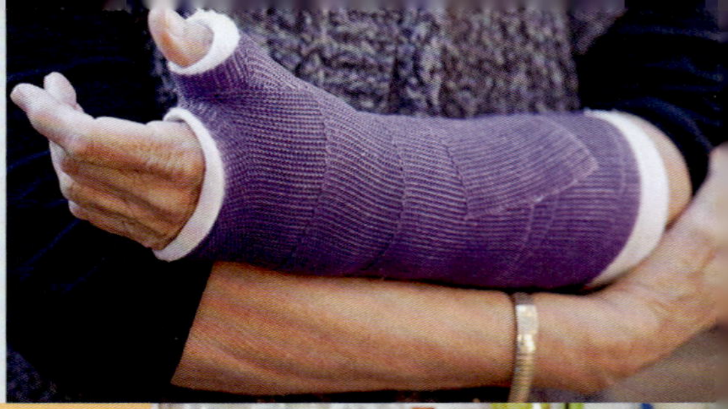

> **Goal:** describe past experiences
> **Grammar:** present perfect with *ever* and *never*
> **Vocabulary:** verb phrases

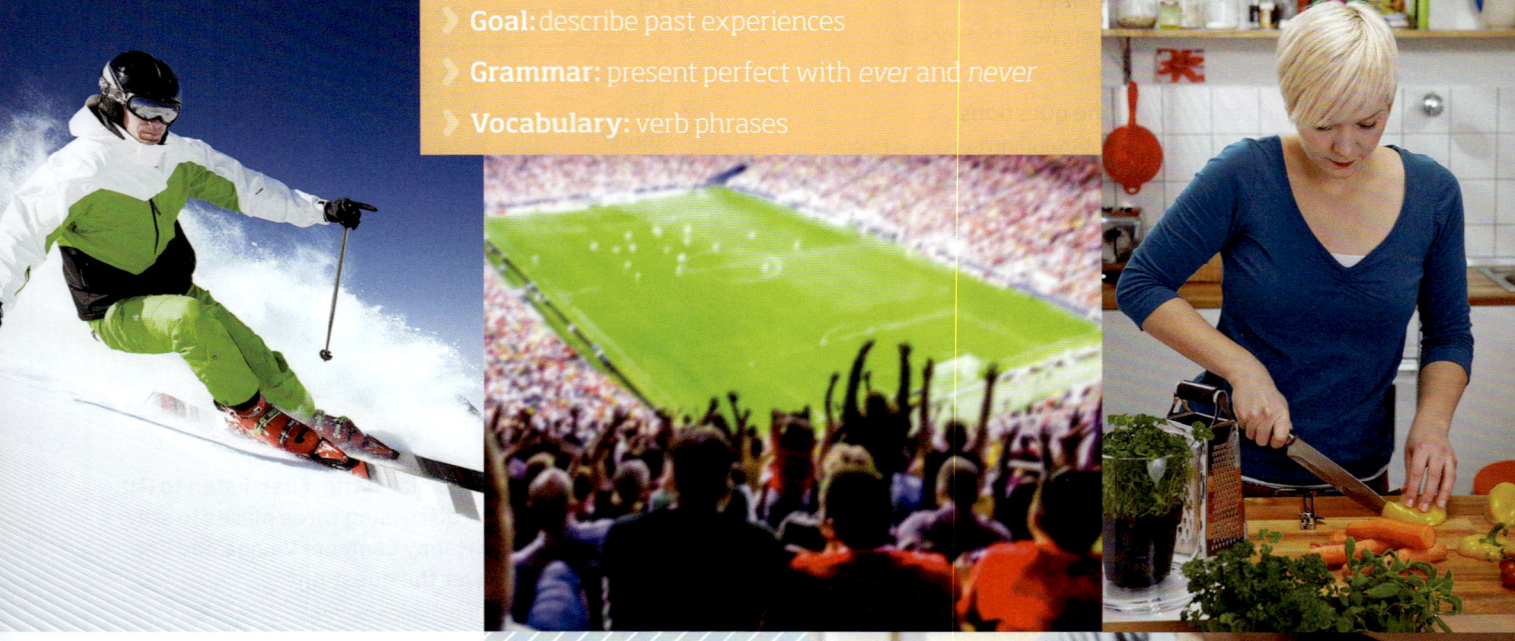

Vocabulary

1 a Work in pairs. Match a verb in box A with a word or phrase in box B. Sometimes more than one answer is possible.

A

| be | break | cook | drive | eat | fall | go | learn |
| ride | share | visit | watch | | | | |

B

an art gallery	asleep in public	a bike	a bone
a football match	a meal	on TV	a photo online
skiing	a sports car	to swim	with chopsticks

b Which activities can you see in the photos?

2 a Work in pairs. Which activities in Exercise 1a do you think most people do in their lives? Which do people not usually do?

b Complete the sentences so they are true for you. Use the activities in Exercise 1a to help you.
1 I often …
2 I never …
3 When I was younger, I …
4 Last year, I …
5 I once …
6 I didn't … until I was … years old.

c Work in pairs. Tell your partner your sentences and give more information.

I often fall asleep on the train. I once missed my station because I was asleep.

Go to your app for more practice.

Listening

3 a 3.5 Listen to a radio show. Which activity does each speaker talk about? What's their reason for not doing it?

b Listen again and choose the correct alternatives.
1 I've never *learn/learnt* to swim.
2 I've never *swim/swum* in the sea.
3 I've never *ride/ridden* a bike.
4 I *saw/seen* my brother fall off his bike and he broke his arm.
5 He's never *watch/watched* a football match in his life.
6 Have you ever *try/tried* to take him to a match?
7 Have you *ever/never* boiled an egg?
8 I've *ever/never* used a cooker.

Grammar

4 Read the grammar box and choose the correct alternatives.

> ### Present perfect with *ever* and *never*
>
> Use the present perfect to talk about things that happened in the past. You ¹*do/don't* say exactly when they happened.
>
> Use *has/have* + ²*infinitive/past participle* to form the present perfect.
>
> He's **seen** lots of tennis matches.
>
> Use the ³*past simple/present perfect simple* to say when something happened.
>
> I **went** to a pool **when** I was in Spain.
>
> Use *never* in a ⁴*statement/question*.
>
> He's **never** watched a football match.
>
> Use *ever* in a ⁵*statement/question*.
>
> Have you **ever** boiled an egg?

5 a 🔊 3.6 Listen to the sentences. Notice the pronunciation of *has/hasn't* and *have/haven't*.

  1 **A:** I've never eaten with chopsticks. Have you?
     B: Yes, I have.
  2 **A:** Sara's broken her arm.
     B: Oh, no! I've never broken a bone.
  3 **A:** Have you ever fallen asleep in public?
     B: No, I haven't.
  4 **A:** Has Max ever cooked a meal for you?
     B: Yes, he has.

b Work in pairs. Listen and repeat.

6 a Complete each sentence with *never* and the present perfect form of a verb in the box.

| drive | eat | learn | meet | ride | share |
| visit | watch | | | | |

  1 I _____ a photo online.
  2 My family and I _____ to swim.
  3 I _____ a motorbike.
  4 I _____ a sports car.
  5 Most of my friends _____ a *Star Wars* film.
  6 I _____ a famous person in real life.
  7 One of my friends _____ a museum.
  8 I _____ caviar.

b Work in pairs. Are any of the sentences true for you? Correct the false ones.

7 a Write three questions with *Have you ever … ?* and the verb phrases in Exercise 1a. Think of two follow-up questions to ask if the answer is *yes*.

b Work in pairs. Take turns to ask and answer your questions.

> **A:** *Have you ever broken a bone?*
> **B:** *Yes, I have.*
> **A:** *What did you break?*

📱 Go to page 120 or your app for more information and practice.

Speaking

PREPARE

8 a 🔊 3.7 You're going to play a game called *Truth or Lie?* First, listen to Amy and Rob playing the game. How does it work?

b Listen again and number Amy's questions in the order you hear them.

  a Why were there cameras in the IT department?
  b What happened?
  c What did you do?
  d When was that? 1
  e How did they make that mistake?

c Work in pairs. Do you think Rob is telling the truth? Why/Why not?

d 🔊 3.8 Listen and check your ideas.

9 Work in pairs. You're going to play *Truth or Lie?* First, make notes about two experiences that you've had and two experiences that you haven't had. For example:

- a meal you've cooked
- a place you've visited
- a prize you've won
- a sport you've played

SPEAK

10 a Play the game with your partner. Take turns to read your sentences and ask questions about them. Decide if your partner's sentences are true or a lie. Use the Useful phrases to help you.

b Play the game with a different partner.

c Who told an interesting true story? Who told an interesting lie?

> **Useful phrases**
> Shall I start?
> It's my/your turn.
> I think that's (true/a lie).
> Well done!

Develop your listening — page 94

3D English in action

Goal: give and respond to news

1. Work in pairs. What kind of news do people usually share with each other? Use the topics below to help you.
   - family
   - friends
   - holidays
   - home
   - interests
   - technology
   - travel
   - work

   People often talk about work or their children.

2. a 3.13 Listen to three conversations. Which topic is each conversation about?

   b Look at the Useful phrases. Then listen to the conversations again. In which conversation 1–3 do you hear each phrase?

   Useful phrases

   Giving news
   Guess what!
   Have you heard about … ?

   Asking for news
   How are things? 1
   How have you been?

   Responding to good news
   That's (brilliant/great/fantastic)!
   That's (fantastic/great/good) news.
   Lucky you!
   Sounds (amazing/brilliant/great)!

   Responding to bad news
   Sorry to hear that.
   What a shame/That's a shame.
   That's (awful/sad/not good).

3. a 3.14 Listen to two different speakers responding to some news. Do you think Speaker 1 or 2 uses the appropriate intonation in each phrase? Why?
   1. Oh, that's a shame.
   2. Really? That's a surprise!
   3. Oh, I'm sorry to hear that
   4. Really? That's not good!
   5. Lucky you!

   b 3.15 Listen and repeat. Copy the intonation.

4. a Read the sentences. Think about how to respond to each one. Use the Useful phrases to help you.
   1. Guess what! I've won a trip to Paris!
   2. Have you heard from Mike? He lost his phone last night!
   3. I'm really sorry. I can't come to your birthday party.
   4. We lost the match yesterday.
   5. How are things with you?
   6. My cat's missing. I can't find him anywhere.
   7. Hey, I've got a new job!
   8. Did you know that Tom's never read a book?

   b Work in pairs. Take turns to read a sentence from Exercise 4a and respond.
   B: Guess what! I've won a trip to Paris!
   A: Lucky you!

Speaking

PREPARE

5. Imagine you're going to meet a friend to share some news. Choose three topics from Exercise 1 and make notes about some good or bad news – it can be real or imagined.

SPEAK

6. a Work in pairs and share your news with each other. Use the Useful phrases to help you.
   A: Hey, how have you been?
   B: Hi! I'm well, thanks. Guess what? I've got a new job!
   A: That's brilliant! What is it?
   B: I'm now head of sales.
   A: Great! I have some good news, too – I've bought a new flat!
   B: That's fantastic news!

   b Work with a different partner and have another conversation.

Go online for the Roadmap video.

Check and reflect

1 a Complete each sentence with an adjective in the box.

> dirty   interesting   lively   modern   noisy   peaceful

1. The air in the city isn't very clean. It's quite _____ .
2. I know you find art galleries boring but I think they're _____ .
3. I like _____ restaurants with lots of people and noise.
4. I prefer _____ cities to old ones.
5. Most places are busy and noisy but the park is _____ .
6. This street's so _____ . I can't hear what you're saying!

b Work in pairs. Which adjectives can you use to describe the area where you are now?

2 a Complete the blog post with comparatives.

These days I live in London but I actually grew up on an island in the south of the UK called the Isle of Wight. The island's about 40 km long and 20 km wide with a population of 130,000 people so it's much ¹_____ (small) than London. London's ²_____ (busy) and ³_____ (noisy) of course but it's also ⁴_____ (interesting) because there are so many things to do. There's a cinema on the island and lots of good places to eat out, but London has ⁵_____ (exciting) nightlife.
I feel lucky because I can enjoy London but also escape to the island for some weekends at the beach. The air there is ⁶_____ (fresh) than in London and I really feel that I can relax. I don't usually go there in summer though because the beaches feel ⁷_____ (crowded) as London! It's ⁸_____ (good) to go in spring or autumn when it's ⁹_____ (busy).

b Work in pairs and compare two places that you know.

3 a Complete each sentence about where you live with a superlative and your own idea.

1. The _____ (good) place to meet new people is _____ .
2. The _____ (nice) time of year is _____ .
3. The _____ (quiet) place in the area is _____ .
4. The _____ (delicious) food around here is _____ .

b Work in pairs. Share your answers to 3a. Do you agree?

4 a Complete the hotel description with the words below.

> airport transfer   breakfast included   five-star
> free parking   organised tours
> room service   sea view   24-hour reception

The Ambassador Hotel is a ¹_____ hotel with excellent service. There is a ²_____ so guests can check in at any time. Our rooms are comfortable and most of them have a ³_____ . There's ⁴_____ in the price and ⁵_____ is available if you want to eat in your room. There's ⁶_____ for people who want to drive here, and we offer a free ⁷_____ when you need to get your flight home. While you're with us, make sure you go on one of our fantastic ⁸_____ around the city to see some of the sights.

b Work in pairs. Describe your dream hotel. Where is it? What is in it? What can you do there?

5 a Choose the correct alternatives.

1. She's so lazy. She *has/have* never worked a day in her life!
2. Have you *ever/never* been to Greece?
3. We've never *saw/seen* so many people on this beach.
4. Luke *been/went* to the Maldives last year.
5. *I never/I've never* had a birthday party when I was a child.
6. *Did/Have* you ever tried sushi?
7. He *have/has* never played basketball.
8. They *spoke/have spoken* to a famous person at the weekend.

b Work in pairs. Take turns to ask *Have you ever ... ?* questions with the activities below and ask some follow-up questions.

- see an elephant
- cook dinner for more than ten people
- play chess
- win a competition
- ride a motorbike

A: *Have you ever seen an elephant?*
B: *Yes, I have.*
A: *When was that?*
B: *Last year in India.*

6 a Complete each sentence with an appropriate verb in the correct form. More than one answer might be possible.

1. I've never _____ on TV but I was once on the radio.
2. My mum's never _____ how to swim.
3. I _____ asleep on the bus yesterday.
4. My brother's never _____ a bike. He prefers walking!
5. Last year I _____ my uncle's sports car. It was fast.
6. I _____ Chinese food for the first time last night.

b Write a list of six activities you think everyone should do in their lifetime.

c Work in pairs and compare your lists. Which activities have you done? Which haven't you done?

Reflect

How confident do you feel about the statements below? Write 1–5 (1 = not very confident, 5 = very confident).

- I can compare places to visit.
- I can choose a place to stay.
- I can describe past expediences.
- I can give and respond to news.

Want more practice?
Go to your Workbook or app.

4A Special days

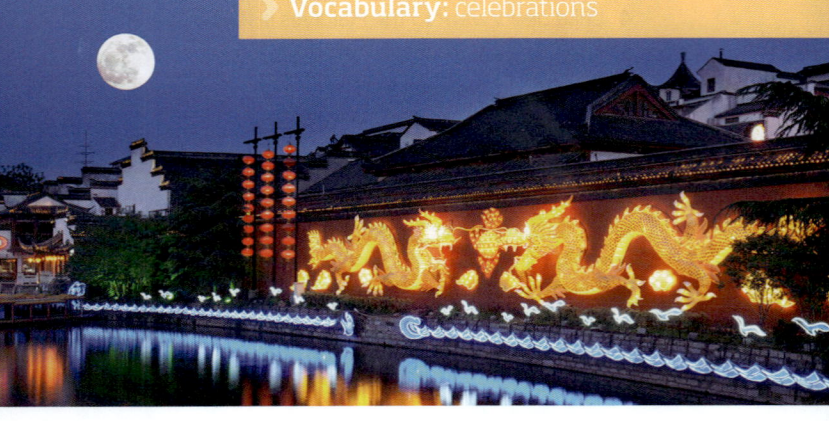

> **Goal:** talk about plans for a special day
> **Grammar:** *be going to, want* and *would like*
> **Vocabulary:** celebrations

Reading and vocabulary

1 Work in pairs and look at the photos. What can you see? Which countries do you think these celebrations happen in?

2 a Read the text and check your ideas in Exercise 1. Match each celebration to a photo.

b Read the article again and answer the questions.
1 When do people celebrate each day?
2 What do people do on these days?
3 On which day do people not go to work?

Celebrations around the WORLD

Friend's Day
Friend's Day in Argentina is on 20th July each year. It's a really important day and people start preparing a long time before. It's not a public holiday so people still work, but in the evenings they meet up with friends. It's popular to go out for a meal and restaurants are always full. People often contact old friends and give gifts to each other.

Moon Festival
This is one of the most famous festivals in China. The date changes every year but people celebrate it every autumn. It happens at this time of year because it's when farmers collect the food from their fields. It's called the Moon Festival because people thank the moon for the seasons and the food. It's a public holiday so people enjoy themselves all day. Some people celebrate at home, others go out to look at the moon, and lots of people eat traditional mooncakes.

Burns Night
Robert Burns was a famous Scottish poet in the 18th century. Every 25th January, on his birthday, friends and family get together to celebrate Burns Night. People work during the day, so in the evening they have dinner parties and invite friends and family to their homes for a Burns Supper. They eat traditional food such as haggis and read some of Robert Burns' poems. They have fun on a cold winter's night.

3 a Complete each question with a word or phrase in the box. Use the text in Exercise 2 to help you.

> celebrate   contact old friends   festivals
> ~~get together~~   give gifts   go out for a meal
> have dinner parties   have fun
> public holiday   traditional

1 How often do you _get together_ with your friends and family?
2 Do you ever _____? How do you find them?
3 Do you like to _____ at your home? Are you a good cook?
4 What's your favourite _____? Does everyone have a day off work?
5 When did you last _____? Where did you go? What did you eat?
6 Do you prefer to _____ or receive them?
7 Are there any good _____ in your area? What do people do at them?
8 How do you like to _____ your birthday?
9 Do you prefer _____ festivals or modern ones?
10 How do you like to _____ and celebrate? What kinds of things do you do?

b Work in pairs and take turns to ask and answer the questions.

Go to your app for more practice.

Grammar

4 a 🔊 **4.1** Listen to Ben and Jane talking about Burns Night. What are their plans?

b Listen again and choose the correct alternatives.
1. I'm *going/want* to invite my neighbours to my house.
2. My mum *would like/'s going* to cook for the whole family.
3. I'd *like/want* to make a traditional meal.
4. I'm *not going/don't want* to cook haggis though.
5. I *would like/want* to ask my neighbours to bring a dessert.
6. What poems *are you going to/do you want* to read?

5 Read the grammar box and choose the correct alternatives.

---
be going to, want and would like
Use *be + going to +* ¹*infinitive/-ing form* to talk about future plans.
I'm going to invite my neighbours for dinner.
Use *want* and *would like +* ²*infinitive/-ing form* to talk about things we want to do.
I'd like to make a traditional meal.
I want to ask my neighbours to bring a dessert.
Use these time expressions to talk about the future:
in an hour, this Friday, next week, in two weeks/in two weeks' time.

---

6 a 🔊 **4.2** Listen to the sentences. Notice the pronunciation of *to* in each one. Is it strong or weak?
1. Dan wants to have a dinner party next week.
2. Kelly's going to contact her old school friends.
3. I'd like to go out for a meal later.

b Listen again and repeat.

7 a Complete the conversation with the correct forms of the verbs in the box.

| be going to/do   ~~be going to/celebrate~~ |
| be going to/have   be going to/get together |
| want/find   would like to/go |

A: Have you had any ideas for Friend's Day? How ¹ _are_ you ² _going to celebrate_ ?
B: I ³ _____ with some old school friends. We ⁴ _____ a dinner.
A: That's nice. Where are you going?
B: We ⁵ _____ to a great restaurant near my flat, if there are any tables available.
A: What ⁶ _____ you ⁷ _____ if it's full?
B: I'm not sure. We ⁸ _____ somewhere nice and quiet so we can chat.
A: Well, Chesco's Pizza is really nice, and in a quiet part of town. You could go there.
B: Great idea! Thanks!

b Work in pairs. Practise the conversation.

8 a Put the future time expressions in order from nearest (1) to furthest (8) in time.
- in two months' time
- next April
- at two o'clock tomorrow
- the day after tomorrow
- the year after next
- in 2060
- in an hour *1*
- this Saturday

b Complete the sentences with your own ideas and a time expression.
1. I'm going …
   I'm going to start a new job next month.
2. I'm not going …
3. I want …
4. I don't want …
5. I'd like …
6. I wouldn't like …

c Work in pairs and compare your sentences. Ask each other questions to find out more.
A: *I'm going to start a new job next month.*
B: *That's great. What are you going to do?*

📱 Go to page 122 or your app for more information and practice.

Speaking

PREPARE

9 You're going to talk about a celebration (e.g. a birthday, a graduation or a public holiday) happening soon. It can be real or imagined. First, make notes and answer the questions.
- When is it?
- What are you going to do?
- Where are you going to celebrate it?
- Who are you going to celebrate with?

SPEAK

10 a Work in groups. Take turns to tell each other about your celebration. Ask each other questions to find out more. Use the Useful phrases to help you.

Useful phrases
A big celebration for me is (my daughter's birthday).
I'm going to have fun (with friends/my family).
We're going to (have a picnic).
I'd also like to (play some games).
What do you (want to do)?

b Who has the most interesting plans in your group? What are they going to do?

Develop your writing page 95

4B Planning events

- **Goal:** organise an event
- **Grammar:** *will/won't* for decisions and offers
- **Vocabulary:** organising events

Reading

1. Work in pairs. Have you ever done any of the things below? Tell your partner about them.
   - cooked a meal for lots of people
   - organised a surprise birthday party
   - organised your own birthday party
   - organised a work event

2. a Work in pairs. How organised are you? Give yourself a score from 1–30 (30 = very organised).

   b Do the quiz. Then go to page 153, add up your score and read your results. Do you agree? Why/Why not?

3. Work in pairs and discuss the questions.
   1. Can you think of any other important things that you have to do when organising an event?
   2. What's the best event you've ever been to? Why was it so good?

Grammar

4. Read the grammar box and choose the correct alternatives.

   ### *will/won't* for decisions and offers

   To make a decision or an offer, use *will* + infinitive ¹*with to/without to*.
   I'll book another restaurant.
   I'll change it if you need me to.
   Will is contracted to *'ll* and *will not* is contracted to *won't*.
   I'll start now.
   I won't organise anything for a month or two.

5. a 🔊 4.3 Listen and choose the sentence you hear.
   1. a I'll drive to work.
      b I drive to work.
   2. a We'll help them clean.
      b We help them clean.
   3. a I'll call Ella every day.
      b I call Ella every day.
   4. a We'll play on Sunday.
      b We play on Sunday.

   b Listen again and repeat.

Are you organised?

1. **Your boss wants you to organise a party for your colleagues in three months' time. What do you think?**
   a I'll start now. It's important to organise everything early.
   b I'll think about some ideas now, but I won't organise anything for a month or two.
   c Three months is a long time. I can forget about it for now.

2. **You want to organise a party to celebrate your dad's birthday, but you don't have any money. What do you think?**
   a I'll get my dad to pay for it. I'll suggest he cooks a meal for everyone or takes us to a restaurant.
   b I'll hire a big room and book a DJ, then sell tickets to pay for it.
   c I'll ask other family members to help with the cost.

3. **You're organising a party in a restaurant for 30 people. Two days before, you find out the restaurant doesn't have any vegetarian options and you know that ten of the people you invited are vegetarians. What do you think?**
   a I'll ask the vegetarians not to come.
   b I'll book another restaurant.
   c I'll speak to the manager and ask them to prepare a vegetarian option. Thirty people is good business for them.

4. **You're organising a sports event and you've got too much to do. You're worried you can't do everything. What do you think?**
   a I'll ask people to help.
   b I'll cancel the event.
   c I'll make it a smaller event, with fewer sports.

5. **You sent out invitations to your friend's surprise birthday party two weeks ago, but no one's replied. What do you think?**
   a 'Why didn't you reply? I'll have to cancel the party now.'
   b 'Did you get the invitation? I'd really like you to come.'
   c 'Is that date difficult for you? I'll change it if you need me to.'

6. **You're organising a big party and two hours before the DJ calls you to say he can't come. What do you think?**
   a 'Don't worry, I've got some music on my phone.'
   b 'Why didn't you tell me earlier? I'll see if my friend can play instead.'
   c 'I won't ever call you again!'

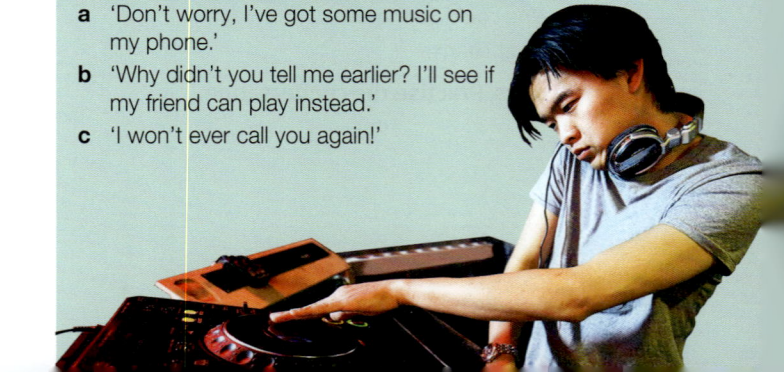

6 Complete the conversations with *'ll* and a verb in the box.

| carry | clean | come | do | make |

1   A: These bags are really heavy.
    B: I _____ them for you.
2   A: Hello Jamie? I've missed the last bus.
    B: Don't worry, I _____ and get you.
3   A: Mum, I'm hungry.
    B: OK, I _____ you a snack.
4   A: Right, we need someone to book the restaurant.
    B: OK, I _____ it – I've got their number.
5   A: What have you done to my car – it's really dirty!
    B: Sorry, we _____ it now.

Go to page 122 or your app for more information and practice.

Vocabulary

7 a Work in pairs. Imagine you're organising a surprise party for someone. Make a list of the things you need to do.

b Complete the 'to do' list with the verbs in the box.

| bake | book | ~~choose~~ | plan | ~~make~~ | remind |
| send | set | | | | |

Kate's party – to do list
1 _____ a date – 30th March?
2 *choose* a place – restaurant? club? town hall?
3 _____ a DJ
4 _____ invitations
5 _____ a cake (chocolate!)
6 *make* some food – lasagne? pizza? sandwiches?
7 _____ activities/things to do – games?
8 _____ people one week before!

c Were any of your ideas in Exercise 7a on the list?

8 Choose the correct alternatives.
A: Right, so we need to ¹*set/plan* a date. Kate's birthday is on 1st April, but that's a Monday. What about having a party on the Saturday before?
B: Sounds good. I'll ²*bake/book* a DJ if you want.
A: Great. We also need to ³*remind/choose* a place. What about the town hall?
C: Good idea. I work near there so I'll book it.
A: OK, I'll ⁴*make/send* invitations to everyone. What about food?
C: Oh, I'll ⁵*plan/bake* a cake! Kate loves chocolate!
B: Yes, and I'll ⁶*make/set* lasagne – it's her favourite.
A: Brilliant. I'll ⁷*send out/plan* some games to play after dinner, too ... OK, anything else?
C: I'll ⁸*remind/choose* everyone a few days before so they don't forget!

Go to your app for more practice.

Speaking

PREPARE

9 a Work in groups. You're going to plan an event together. First, decide what kind of event you want to organise. Use the ideas below or think of your own idea.
- a birthday party
- a class party to celebrate the end of the course
- a work summer party
- a sports event
- a music festival

b Make a 'to do' list of things you need to organise.

SPEAK

10 Organise your event. Decide who will do what and when they will do it. Use the Useful phrases to help you.

> **Useful phrases**
> We need to (send out invitations).
> I'll (book a band) if you want.
> Can you (call the restaurant)?
> What about (food and drink)?

11 Tell the class about your event.
We're going to have a party for Ana's birthday. Marcelo's going to bake a cake.

Develop your listening page 96

4B | Planning events

33

4c Rules of the race

> **Goal:** present an idea for an event
> **Grammar:** *can* and *have to*
> **Vocabulary:** *-ed* and *-ing* adjectives

Listening

1 a Have you ever taken part in a race or do you know someone else who has? What kind of race was it?

  b Read about an extreme race. Which of the activities can you see in the photos? Why do you think people want to do this race?

THE MASSIVE MUD RUN

Run a 5 km course as many times as you can over 12 hours. And while you're running you'll also:
- climb over walls
- swim through muddy water
- jump over fire

Come and join the FUN!

2 4.7 Listen to Felicity asking her colleague Lucas about the race. Answer the questions.

  1 Which things in the box does Felicity ask about?

  | breaks | cost | health | location | start time |
  | teams | visitors | what to wear | | |

  2 Does Felicity decide to run in the race?

3 a Listen again and tick (✓) the statements that are true.
  You need to ...
  1 be very fit.
  2 see a doctor before the race.
  3 do all parts of the race.
  4 wear special clothes.
  It's possible to ...
  5 bring food.
  6 have a rest during the race.
  7 run in a team.
  8 get your money back after paying.

  b 4.8 Listen to the extracts and complete the sentences.
  1 Do I _____ to be very fit?
  2 You don't have _____ see a doctor before you do it but it's a good idea.
  3 Runners _____ to do everything on the course.
  4 You _____ have to wear any special clothes.
  5 _____ people bring their own food?
  6 _____ I have a rest during the race?
  7 But if you don't want to run on your own, you _____ run in a team.
  8 After you pay, you _____ get your money back.

  c Work in pairs and discuss the questions.
  1 Would you like to take part in a race like this?
  2 Do you know about any other unusual races?

Grammar

4 Complete the grammar box with *can*, *can't*, *have to* and *don't have to*. Use Exercise 3b to help you.

can and have to

Obligation
Use [1]_____ to say that something is necessary.
*Runners **have to** do everything on the course.*
Use [2]_____ to say that something is not necessary.
*You **don't have to** see a doctor before the race.*

Possibility
Use [3]_____ to talk about things that are possible.
*You **can** run in a team.*
Use [4]_____ to talk about things that are not possible.
*After you pay, you **can't** get your money back.*

5 a 🔊 4.9 **Listen to the sentences. When are *can* and *can't* stressed/not stressed?**

1 **A:** Can I take my own food?
   B: Yes, you can.
2 **A:** Can we get our money back?
   B: No, we can't.
3 **A:** Can we run together in a team?
   B: Yes, we can.

b Listen again and repeat.

6 a Complete the descriptions with *can, can't, have to* or *don't have to* in the correct form and the verb in brackets.

Unusual RACES around the WORLD

1 Every May, in the UK, someone throws a cheese from the top of Cooper's Hill and runners ¹_____ (try) and catch it. There ²_____ (be) more than 15 runners in a race because people often fall down and have accidents.

2 The Colorado Pack Burro race is a marathon with a difference. Each runner ³_____ (take) a donkey up a 29-mile path. However, there's one important rule – they ⁴_____ (push) the donkey, pull the donkey or even carry the donkey, but they can't ride it.

3 In the wife-carrying race in Finland, runners ⁵_____ (carry) their wives along a 253.5 metre track. The wife ⁶_____ (run) at all, only the man can. She ⁷_____ (be) the runner's own wife – it's OK if she's a friend's wife, for example.

b Which race do you think is the most unusual?

7 a Complete the sentences so they are true for you.
1 Most days, I have to …
2 I don't have to …
3 Usually, I can …
4 I can't …

b Work in pairs. Tell each other your sentences and ask some questions.
   A: *Most days, I have to get up at 5.30.*
   B: *Why do you have to do that?*

📱 Go to page 122 or your app for more information and practice.

Vocabulary

8 a Which of the adjectives in bold in sentences 1–4 describe a feeling and which describe a thing?
1 I'm **interested** in running the Massive Mud Run.
2 It's an **interesting** course.
3 The race is really **tiring**.
4 The race lasts 12 hours so you'll be **tired**.

b Choose the correct alternatives.
1 Which sports do you think are *bored/boring*?
2 Do you feel *relaxed/relaxing* after you do exercise?
3 When was the last time you were *excited/exciting* about a sport?
4 What *interested/interesting* things do you enjoy doing?
5 What do you sometimes feel *worrying/worried* about?
6 What's the most *tiring/tired* thing you've ever done?
7 What's the most *excited/exciting* sporting moment in your country's history?
8 What's the most *surprised/surprising* thing someone has done for you?

c Work in pairs. Take turns to ask and answer the questions in Exercise 8b.

📱 Go to page 139 or your app for more vocabulary and practice.

Speaking

PREPARE

9 a 🔊 4.10 You're going to present an idea for a race. First, listen to Marco and his classmates presenting their idea. Who is the race for?

b Listen again and answer the questions.
1 Where is the race?
2 Do the runners run alone or in teams?
3 Do the runners have to wear anything special?
4 What are the rules of the race?
5 What prizes do the winners get?

10 Work in groups. Plan a race for your town or city.

SPEAK

11 a Present your race to the class. Use the Useful phrases to help you.

b Vote for the best idea. You can't vote for your own!

Useful phrases
The (event) is (in June).
The winners get (a prize).
It starts at (9 a.m.) in Dublin.
(Runners) have to/don't have to/can/can't (bring water).

Develop your reading
page 97

4C | Rules of the race

35

4D English in action

Goal: make plans to meet

Listening

1 **Look at photos A–C and answer the questions.**
   1 How often do you do these things with your friends?
   2 What other things do you like to do?
   3 How do you organise to meet?
   4 How often do you do the things in the photos?

2 a **4.11 Listen to conversations 1–3 and match each one to the places in photos A–C.**

   b **Listen again and answer the questions.**
   1 Why doesn't Lucy want to meet at the park entrance?
   2 Where do Lucy and Susan decide to meet?
   3 Why can't Jimmy meet on Friday?
   4 Why can't Chris meet on Sunday?
   5 Why doesn't Tanya want to go to the concert by taxi?
   6 Why does Paul think this isn't a problem?

3 **Look at the Useful phrases and then listen again. In which conversation (1, 2 or 3) do you hear the phrases in the box?**

> **Useful phrases**
>
> **Inviting people**
> Would you like to come? *1*
> Do you want to meet up (this Friday)?
> Do you want to join us?
>
> **Responding to invitations**
> I'd love to!
> Yes, that sounds (fun/great).
> I don't think I can, sorry.
> I'm sorry I can't, I'm busy.
>
> **Organising when and where to meet**
> Where/What time shall we meet?
> Shall we meet (at ten/at the park)?
> Let's meet (in front of the bank/at five o'clock).
>
> **Responding to suggestions**
> That's a good idea.
> I'm not sure about that.

4 a **4.12 Listen to the phrases and underline the stressed words.**
   1 Would you like to come?
   2 Do you want to join us?
   3 I'd love to.
   4 Where shall we meet?
   5 Shall we meet at ten?
   6 That's a good idea.

   b **Listen again and repeat.**

5 a **Use the prompts to write questions.**
   1 like / go / cinema / tomorrow?
   2 want / play football / us / weekend?
   3 Shall / go / a restaurant?
   4 time / shall / meet?
   5 Shall / meet / seven o'clock?

   b **Work in pairs. Practise saying the questions and responding in different ways.**

Speaking

PREPARE

6 **You're going to organise something to do with your classmates. First, make notes about what you'd like to do (e.g. have lunch, go for a run). Answer the questions below to help you.**
   • What are you going to do?
   • What time would you like to meet?
   • Where would you like to meet?

SPEAK

7 a **Go around the class and invite people to meet up. Respond to other people's invitations. Use the Useful phrases to help you.**
   A: Would you like to come to our picnic?
   B: I'd love to. Where is it?
   A: It's in Parco Centrale. It starts at one o'clock.

   b **Did you make any interesting plans? Which Useful phrases did you find the most useful?**

Go online for the Roadmap video.

Check and reflect

1 a **Find five mistakes and correct them.**
   1 I'm going move to another country after I graduate.
   2 I'd like to go away somewhere nice this weekend.
   3 I going to finish this lesson in 30 minutes.
   4 My parents want retire when they're 70.
   5 I'm going to have dinner at eight o'clock tonight.
   6 I like to visit Denmark one day.
   7 The teacher's going to give us lots of homework.
   8 Two of my friends is going to get married next year.

   b **Change the sentences so that they're true for you.**
   1 I'm going to move to Istanbul next year.

2 **Match the halves of each phrase.**
   1 public   a gifts
   2 go out   b holiday
   3 give   c old friends
   4 have   d for a meal
   5 have a dinner e together
   6 contact   f fun
   7 get   g party

3 **Work in pairs and discuss the questions.**
   1 What was the last special day you celebrated?
   2 Which of the things in Exercise 2 did you do?

4 a **Choose the correct alternatives.**
   1 I'll *carry/to carry* it for you.
   2 *I won't/I'll* pick you up if you want.
   3 We'll *looking/look* after the kids tonight.
   4 I'll *lend/to lend* you some money.
   5 *I/I'll* help her.

   b **Work in pairs. What do you think the other person says before each offer in Exercise 4a?**

5 **Put the sentences and questions in the correct order.**
   1 party / I'd / Sam's / go / to / to / like
   2 you / do / go / to / running / want / ?
   3 August / to / this / Mark's / Ibiza / going
   4 Saturday / are / watch / on / you / to / going / match / the / ?
   5 dinner / come / she'll / after / home
   6 tonight / I'm / late / going / stay / to / out / not
   7 doesn't / to / change / Kate / want / job / her
   8 world / like / would / the / you / travel / around / to / ?

6 **Complete the sentences with the missing word.**
   1 I need to p_____ some games for my son's fifth birthday.
   2 Let's b_____ a cake for Ella's birthday.
   3 My mum always m_____ a special dish at New Year.
   4 I'm going to s_____ the invitations next week.
   5 Did you r_____ everyone about the party?
   6 Have they s_____ a date for their wedding?

7 **Work in pairs. Think of the last time you planned an event. Tell each other what you did.**

8 a **Complete the sports rules with *can, can't, have to* or *don't have to*.**
   1 Football: You _____ touch the ball with your feet, legs and head but you _____ touch it with your hands.
   2 Running: You _____ use any special equipment, but there are lots of things you _____ use if you want to.
   3 Swimming: You _____ use your body to move through the water.
   4 Tennis: You _____ hit a ball with a racket.
   5 Basketball: You _____ touch the ball with your hands but you _____ carry the ball while you move.
   6 Golf: You _____ hit the ball into a hole. You _____ kick it with your foot or move it with your hand.
   7 Volleyball: You _____ to hit the ball over the net with your hands. You _____ use your feet or head. You _____ play it on the beach.

   b **Work in pairs. Think of another sport. What are the rules?**

9 a **Choose the correct alternatives.**
   1 I feel *worried/worrying* a lot about work.
   2 I think horror films are very *frightened/frightening*.
   3 I'd like to be more *relaxed/relaxing* about speaking English.
   4 I was *surprised/surprising* when I read the news yesterday.
   5 I think surfing is *excited/exciting*.
   6 I'm not very *interested/interesting* in sport.
   7 I never feel *bored/boring* when I'm at work.
   8 For me, shopping is a really *tired/tiring* activity.

   b **Change the sentences so they're true for you.**

Reflect

How confident do you feel about the statements below? Write 1–5 (1 = not very confident, 5 = very confident).
- I can describe plans.
- I can organise an event.
- I can present an idea for an event.
- I can make plans to meet.

Want more practice?
Go to your Workbook or app.

5A The right person

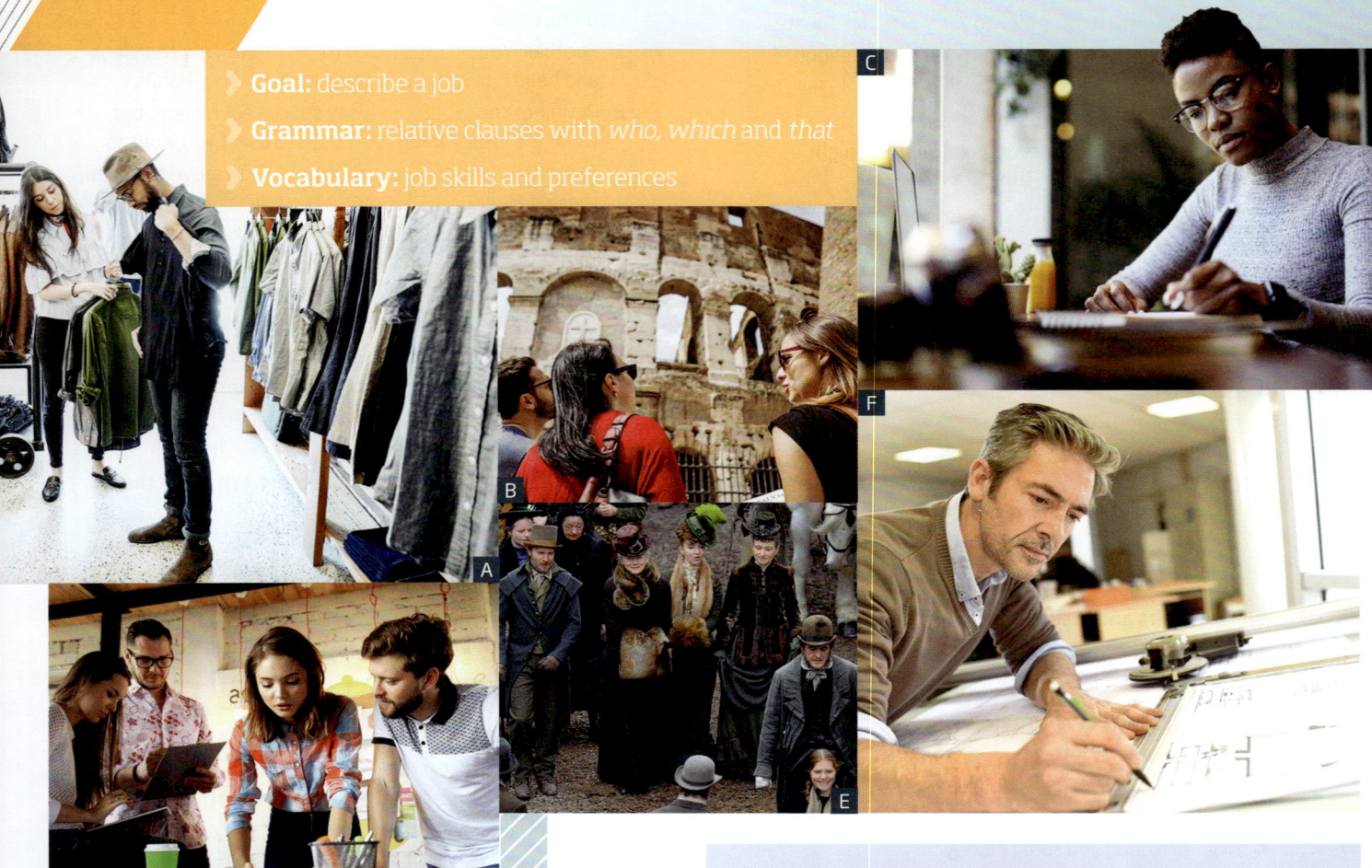

> **Goal:** describe a job
> **Grammar:** relative clauses with *who, which* and *that*
> **Vocabulary:** job skills and preferences

Vocabulary and listening

1 a Work in pairs. How many jobs can you think of? Write a list.

b Match the jobs in the box with photos A–F.

| architect | businessperson | film extra |
| shop assistant | tour guide | writer |

2 a Read the questionnaire and check you understand the phrases in bold. Then complete the questionnaire for you.

b Work in pairs. Compare your answers to the questionnaire. Do you have the same skills? Do you have similar work habits?

c Work in pairs and discuss the jobs in Exercise 1b.
1 Which jobs can you match with the sentences in the questionnaire?
2 Which jobs would you be good at? Why?
3 Which jobs would you like to do? Why?

Go to page 140 or your app for more vocabulary and practice.

Work and skills questionnaire

Mark the line with a cross to show how much you agree.

1 I am **creative**.
   Disagree ·········· Agree
2 I have **good communication skills**.
   Disagree ·········· Agree
3 I am a **good manager**.
   Disagree ·········· Agree
4 I like **working in a team**.
   Disagree ·········· Agree
5 I like **working from home**.
   Disagree ·········· Agree
6 I like **working on my own**.
   Disagree ·········· Agree
7 I'd like to **work part-time**.
   Disagree ·········· Agree
8 I don't need **a job that is well-paid**.
   Disagree ·········· Agree
9 I enjoy **working with customers**.
   Disagree ·········· Agree
10 I don't mind **working long hours**.
   Disagree ·········· Agree

3 a 🔊 **5.1** Listen to Cheryl talking to her friend James. Which of the jobs in Exercise 1b do they mention? Which job does Cheryl like?

b Listen again and answer the questions.
1. Why is Cheryl looking for a new job?
2. What's important for her in a job?
3. Why doesn't she like the first two jobs that James suggests?
4. Why does she like the last job he suggests?

4 🔊 **5.2** Listen to the extracts and choose the correct alternatives.
1. I'd like a job *that's/who's* completely different.
2. I want a job *which/that* is interesting.
3. They want someone *who/which* enjoys writing.
4. Well, they're looking for someone *that/who* can work part-time.

Grammar

5 Read the grammar box and choose the correct alternatives.

Relative clauses with *who*, *which* and *that*

Use defining relative clauses to give more information about people and things.
Use *who* for [1]*people/things*.
*We need **someone who** has good communication skills.*
Use *which* or *that* for [2]*people/things*.
*I want a **teaching job which** is well-paid.*
*She wants a **part-time job that** is interesting.*
It is sometimes possible to use *that* instead of *who*.
He's the man that we interviewed last week.
Also use defining relative clauses to combine two sentences.
He's a doctor. He works all over the world.
= *He's **a doctor who works** all over the world.*

6 a 🔊 **5.3** Listen to the relative clauses and notice the pronunciation of *who*, *which* and *that*.
1. This job is for people who can work long hours.
2. I'd like a job which is interesting.
3. He wants a job that's well-paid.

b Listen again and repeat.

7 Complete the sentences with a relative pronoun.
1. This is the dress _____ I bought yesterday.
2. He's the man _____ fixed my computer.
3. This is the book _____ I read on holiday.
4. It's a job _____ you have to do at night.
5. She's the girl _____ lives next to me.
6. I like films _____ are about real people.
7. Paul is the person _____ told me about this restaurant.
8. This is the time of year _____ I like the best.

8 Choose the correct alternatives to complete the text. What job does it describe?

For this job we need someone [1]*which/who* is creative, so that they can plan activities [2]*who/that* are interesting for small children. The best person for this job is someone [3]*who/which* has good communication skills, because it's a job [4]*who/that* involves working with many different types of people, such as children, parents and managers. It's a job [5]*who/which* isn't usually well-paid, but it's very interesting. Nowadays, you also need to be someone [6]*which/who* is good with computers to do this job well.

9 Work in pairs. Take turns to describe a type of job you would like to do. Use the phrases in the questionnaire to help you. Suggest some jobs for your partner.
A: *I'd like a job which I can do from home.*
B: *How about an online teacher?*

📱 Go to page 124 or your app for more information and practice.

Speaking

PREPARE

10 You're going to describe a job for other students to guess. First, think of a job that you want to describe. Then complete the sentences below.
- It's a job which …
- It isn't a job that you …
- You need to be someone who …
- You can't be someone who likes/doesn't like …

It's a job that you can do at home. You need to be someone who's creative … (an artist).

SPEAK

11 a Work in groups. Describe your job to the group. Can they guess which job you're describing?

b Would you like to do the jobs that other people described? Why/Why not? Use the Useful phrases to help you.

Useful phrases
I'd like to be (a chef) because (I love food).
I wouldn't like to be a (journalist) because I don't like (writing).
I think I'd like this job because (it's creative)
I don't think I'd like this job because (it's not well-paid).

Develop your reading page 98

5A | The right person

39

5B Appearances

> **Speaking:** describe people
> **Grammar:** *look like*, *look* +adjective, *be like*
> **Vocabulary:** appearance

Reading

1 Work in pairs and discuss the questions.
1. Do you use social media? What for?
2. Do you post photos on social media?
3. Have you ever tried to find anyone/anything using social media? Do you think social media is a good way to do this?

2 Read the post and answer the questions.
1. What did Gabriela find?
2. Where did she find it?
3. What does Gabriela want people to do?
4. Who does Katie think the person in the photo is?
5. How does Katie describe Eduardo's personality?

Gabriela Garcia
Hi everyone. I found a camera on Corona Avenue at about 3.00 p.m. today. This is the most recent photo on it. Does anyone know these people? Please share this post so we can find out whose camera it is. Thanks!

Katie Novak
The man in the middle looks like Eduardo's brother, but I'm not sure. You can ask Eduardo – he works in the library.

Gabriela Garcia
I don't know Eduardo. What does he look like?

Katie Novak
He's got dark hair and a beard like the man in the photo, but he doesn't look old. He looks around 35.

Gabriela Garcia
What's he like? Will he think I'm strange if I show him a photo and ask if it's his brother?!

Katie Novak
No, don't worry, he won't think you're strange. He's really nice.

Grammar

3 Read the grammar box and choose the correct alternatives.

look like, *look* + adjective, *be like*

Use *look like* + **¹**adjective/noun to describe people and things that are similar.
*The man in the middle **looks like Eduardo's brother**.*
Use *look* + **²**adjective/noun to describe appearances and feelings.
*You all **look** (really) **happy** in the photo.*
Use *look* + **³**noun/number to say how old we think someone or something is.
*He **looks** (around) **35**.*
Use *What do/does (he/she/they) look like?* to ask about the **⁴**appearance/character of a person or thing.
A: *What does he look like?*
B: *He's got dark hair and a beard.*
Use *What is/are (he/she/they) like?* to ask about a person's **⁵**appearance/character.
A: *What's he like?*
B: *He's lovely.*

4 a 🔊 5.4 Listen to the sentences. What do you notice about the letters in bold?
1. Oh dear. You loo**k a**ngry!
2. He look**s r**eally sad.
3. She look**s l**ike a runner.
4. They loo**k e**xcited.

b Listen again and repeat.

Vocabulary

6 a Match the words in the box with the categories below.

> bald   beard   blonde   casual   curly   dark
> long   moustache   slim   smart   straight
> tall   tattoo

- clothes
- body
- face
- hair

b Think of some more words for each category.

c Work in pairs and compare your ideas.

7 a 🔊 5.5 Listen to Marcus telling Alessia about his family. Tick (✓) the words in Exercise 6a that he uses to describe them.

b Listen again. Make notes about what each member of Marcus's family looks like.

c Work in pairs and compare your notes. Then go to page 154 and check your ideas.

8 a Work in pairs. Look at photos A–F and take turns to describe one of the people. Try to guess which person your partner is describing.

> *This person has short, dark hair and a moustache.*

b Make some guesses about each person's job, age and character with your partner. Use *looks* and *looks like*.

> *A: The man in photo C looks like a rock star.*
> *B: Yes, he looks quite creative.*

c Go to page 154 and read about each person. Did you guess correctly? Is there any surprising information?

📱 Go to your app for more practice.

Speaking

PREPARE

9 You're going to describe three people who are important to you. First, make notes about the things below.
- who each person is
- why each person is important to you
- each person's appearance
- each person's character
- each person's job, interests, etc.
- who each person is similar or different to

SPEAK

10 Work in pairs. Take turns to describe the people you want to talk about. Ask your partner questions. How similar or different are the people you described?

> *A: I want to talk about my friend, Ella. We aren't very similar, but she's really important to me because she's my oldest friend.*
> *B: That's great! Where did you meet her?*

5 a Match the sentence halves.
1. I don't know Tom. What does
2. Is Sam OK? He doesn't
3. I don't think Evan is 30. He
4. The new manager started today. What's
5. Has Cecile had some good news? She
6. What's your dad's job? He

a. he like?
b. looks really happy.
c. look well.
d. looks like a businessperson.
e. looks about 25.
f. he look like?

b Complete the questions and answers with the correct form of *be, like, look* and *look like*.
1. **A:** What does he look like?
   B: He _____ quite young and he has really short hair.
2. **A:** Does she _____ anyone in her family?
   B: Yes, like her dad.
3. **A:** How old does he _____ ?
   B: He looks about 40.
4. **A:** What's she like?
   B: She _____ really nice.
5. **A:** Does she ____ like her twin sister?
   B: Yes, they look exactly the same.
6. **A:** Is she like her brother?
   B: Yes, they ____ both very funny.
7. **A:** What's your new boss ____?
   B: He's very nice!
8. **A:** How old is Anthony?
   B: I don't know, but he ____ really young.

📱 Go to page 124 or your app for more information and practice.

Develop your listening page 99

41

5c Shopping tips

> **Goal:** give advice about shopping
> **Grammar:** *should, shouldn't* and imperatives
> **Vocabulary:** shopping

Vocabulary

1 Look at photos A–E and discuss the questions.
  1 What do you usually buy in these places?
  2 Where do you like to go shopping? Why?
  3 Do you prefer shopping alone or with someone else?
  4 Have you ever had a problem with something you've bought?

2 Work in pairs. Read the shopping tips and check you understand the meaning of the phrases in bold. Do you agree with the tips? Why/Why not?

TOP shopping tips

- **Pay by credit card** – you can collect points!
- Always **ask for a discount**.
- Always **keep the receipt**.
- If you don't have much time when buying clothes, don't **try them on** in the shop. You can always **return something** later (if you kept the receipt!)
- When buying electronic products, **read reviews** first.
- **Compare prices** before you buy – you might find something cheaper **in a sale**.

3 a Complete the questions with the phrases from Exercise 2.
  1 Do you prefer to _____ or in cash? Why?
  2 When is the best time to buy something _____ in your country? Are things a lot cheaper?
  3 When was the last time you had to _____ to a shop? What was the problem?
  4 Do you often _____ or do you usually just pay full price?
  5 Do you _____ after you buy something? Or do you throw it away?
  6 Do you like to _____ ? Do you think other people's opinions are important?
  7 Do you use any websites to _____ ? Do you think this is a good way to save money?
  8 When you buy clothes, do you always _____ first?

b Work in pairs and ask and answer the questions.

Go to your app for more practice.

Listening

4 a You're going to listen to Jenny and Luke describing problems with a coffee machine and a shirt. What kinds of problems do you think they'll describe?

b 🔊 5.9 Listen and check your ideas. Who bought each product? What was each person's problem?

c Listen again and answer the questions.
1. Was the coffee machine that Jenny bought cheap?
2. How much cheaper was the coffee machine on another day?
3. What happened to Luke's shirt on the morning of his interview?
4. Why didn't Luke try the shirt on before he bought it?
5. What was wrong with the shirt?

5 Who gives each piece of advice? Write Jenny (J) or Luke (L).
1. You should always try clothes on in the shop.
2. You shouldn't just buy the first thing you see.
3. Keep the receipt.

6 Work in pairs and discuss the questions.
1. Whose problem do you think was the worst? Why?
2. Have you ever had any problems like these?
3. Do you agree with their advice? Why/Why not?

Grammar

7 Read the grammar box and choose the correct alternatives.

should/shouldn't and imperatives

Use *should* + infinitive to say something is a
¹*good/bad* idea.
You **should ask** for a discount.
Use *shouldn't* + infinitive to say something is a
²*good/bad* idea.
You **shouldn't buy** something if you're not sure about it.
Use an imperative for ³*strong/weak* advice. Make imperatives with the infinitive ⁴*with to/without to*.
Look for sales!
It's also possible to use *always* or *never* before an infinitive.
Never pay by credit card.

8 a 🔊 5.10 Listen to the advice. Is *should* or *shouldn't* stressed?
1. You should ask for a discount.
2. You shouldn't pay the full price.
3. You should return it.
4. You shouldn't buy a used phone.
5. You should read the description carefully.
6. You shouldn't buy that online.

b Listen again and repeat.

9 a Put the words in the correct order to make sentences.
1. old / an / Never / car / buy
2. clothes / buy / online / Don't
3. something / always / you / before / should / You / it / try / buy
4. the / supermarket / discount / Always / a / ask / for / in
5. things / You / cash / pay / expensive / shouldn't / for / in
6. market / buy / You / food / fresh / a / should / from

b Work in pairs. Do you agree with the advice? Why/Why not?

10 a Choose one of the topics below and write three tips for it.
- buying a mobile phone
- buying clothes
- buying a new car
- finding something in a sale
- shopping in your city
- shopping online

b Work in groups. Read out your tips to other students. Can the others guess which topic they're for? Do you agree? Why/Why not?

📱 Go to page 124 or your app for more information and practice.

Speaking

PREPARE

11 You're going to talk about a shopping experience you've had. It can be real or imagined. First, answer the questions below.
- What did you buy/want to buy?
- Was it a good or bad experience?
- Why was it good/bad?
- What happened?
- What advice would you give to someone in the same situation?

SPEAK

12 Work in groups. Tell each other about your experiences and give your advice. Then agree on the two best pieces of advice.

Develop your writing
page 100

5D English in action

> **Goal:** make and respond to suggestions

Listening

1. **Look at the photos and discuss the questions.**
   1. Which item would you most like to receive as a gift?
   2. Are you good at finding gifts for people? Why/Why not?

2. a 🔊 5.11 **Listen to Simon and Tina. Who are they buying gifts for? Why?**

   b **Match the sentence halves. Use the Useful phrases to help you.**

1	How	a	him some gardening books.
2	What about	b	some jewellery?
3	You could get	c	the department store on West Street.
4	Why don't	d	about some flowers?
5	Why don't we	e	you get him a nice sun hat?
6	Let's try	f	go shopping together at the weekend?

   ### Useful phrases

   Making suggestions
   How/What about (some flowers)?
   Why don't you/we (get her a watch)?
   You could (buy him a ball).
   Let's (get something on Saturday).

   Responding to suggestions
   Great!
   (That's a really) good/fantastic idea.
   Maybe/Perhaps.
   I think I'd prefer to (get some flowers).

   c **Listen again and check your answers.**

3. a 🔊 5.12 **Listen to the suggestions. Which word is the most stressed in each one?**
   1. Why don't we make him a cake?
   2. You could get her a book.
   3. Why don't you buy them a game?
   4. What about a new pair of trainers?
   5. I think I'd prefer to get her some chocolates.

   b **Listen again and repeat.**

4. a **Complete each suggestion with an appropriate idea.**
   1. **A:** I'd like to buy my English teacher a gift.
      B: How about _some chocolates_ ?
   2. **A:** What shall we do after class?
      B: Let's _____ .
   3. **A:** I need to get to class but my car won't start.
      B: Why don't you _____ ?
   4. **A:** What shall we have for dinner?
      B: What about _____ ?
   5. **A:** It's my friend's birthday but I don't have much money.
      B: You could _____ .

   b **Work in pairs. Take turns to read the sentences from Exercise 4a and respond with suggestions.**

5. **Work in groups. Take turns to tell each other about a person you'd like to buy a gift for. Give suggestions.**
   A: I'd like to buy a present for my friend Greg. He loves football.
   B: Which team does he like? You could buy him their shirt!

Speaking

PREPARE

6. **Work in pairs. Student A go to page 151 and Student B go to page 155. Follow the instructions.**

SPEAK

7. **Have a conversation and give each other gift suggestions. Try to use as many of the Useful phrases as possible.**
   A: I need to buy a gift for Gail. She's 50, she's a doctor and she likes running. Do you have any ideas?
   B: What about some nice running socks?

Go online for the Roadmap video.

Check and reflect

1 a Choose the correct alternatives.
1 A tour guide is a person *who/which* shows people around a city.
2 Police officers do a job *who/that* is sometimes dangerous.
3 I have a job *which/who* I like.
4 That's the man I *which/who* I work with.
5 Teaching is a job *who/which* is important.

b Write some definitions for jobs using *who* and *which*.

c Work in groups. Read out your definitions. The other students guess what you're describing.
   A: *It's a person who looks after your teeth.*
   B: *Is it a dentist?*
   A: *Yes!*

2 a Match the sentence halves.
1 It's a   a well-paid job.
2 You need to be a good   b a team.
3 You need to be   c manager.
4 Most people who do   d creative.
  this job like working in e from home.
5 People who do this job
  usually work

b Think of a job for each sentence.

3 a Choose the correct alternatives.
1 What does your closest friend *like/look like*?
2 What's your neighbour *like/look like*?
3 Who in your family *are/do* you look like?
4 What *was/were* you like when you were a child?
5 What did you *like/look like* when you were young?

b Match questions 1–5 to answers a–e.
a I was shy and didn't talk much.
b He's a nice man. I like him.
c She's tall with dark hair. She wears glasses.
d I had longer hair ... and I was thinner!
e My son. We have similar faces.

c Work in pairs. Take turns to ask and answer the questions in Exercise 3a.

4 Complete the description with the words in the box.

| curly | fair | moustache | slim | tall |

People say my brother Nik and I look similar, but I don't agree. Nik's ¹_____ but I'm short. He's got dark hair but mine's ²_____ – also, his is straight but mine's ³_____ . He's got a ⁴_____ but I haven't. One thing we do have in common is that we run a lot, so we're both quite ⁵_____ .

5 a Sheila needs to buy a nice dress for a wedding but she hasn't got enough money. Complete the advice with the words in the box.

| don't   make   should (x3)   shouldn't   tell |

1 You _____ explain the situation to your friend. I'm sure she won't mind what you wear.
2 _____ your friend that you can't go. _____ waste your money!
3 You _____ buy new clothes. You _____ look for some nice used clothes.
4 You _____ go online and find a website that sells cheap clothes, or _____ a dress yourself!

b Work in pairs. Can you think of any other advice for Sheila?

6 a Choose the correct alternatives.
1 I never really compare *money/prices* before I buy something.
2 Most people I know pay *by/on* credit card.
3 I keep the *recipe/receipt* for most things that I buy.
4 I never *put/try* on clothes before I buy them.
5 I often ask for *sales/discount*s.
6 I often buy something and then *return/try* it to the shop the next day.
7 I prefer to buy clothes in a *bargain/sale*.

b Work in pairs. Which sentences do you agree with?

7 a Match words in the box to the definitions.

| bald   casual   a discount   work part-time good communication skills |

1 a price which is lower than usual
2 the ability to speak to other people so they understand you well
3 without hair
4 work for only a few days a week
5 informal clothes/style

b Work in pairs. Choose three words or phrases from this unit. Take turns to give a definition and guess the word/phrase.

Reflect

How confident do you feel about the statements below? Write 1–5 (1 = not very confident, 5 = very confident).
- I can describe a job.
- I can describe people.
- I can give advice about shopping.
- I can make and respond to suggestions.

Want more practice?
Go to your Workbook or app.

1A Develop your listening

> **Goal:** understand a short talk
> **Focus:** understanding the main idea

1 a Which greetings below can you see in photos A–F.
- bow your head
- hug someone
- kiss someone on the cheek
- put your hands together
- shake hands
- show your tongue
- press your noses together
- touch someone's hand or arm
- put your hand on your chest

b Do you know which countries the different greetings are from? If not, can you guess?

c 🔊 1.3 Listen to the introduction of a radio programme. Which greetings in Exercise 1a does the radio presenter talk about?

2 Read the Focus box. How can you identify key words?

Understanding the main idea
It isn't always necessary to understand every word when you listen — you can use key words (e.g. verbs, adverbs, nouns, adjectives) to understand the main idea.
It's easier to hear key words when listening because they are usually stressed.
People around the **world greet** each other **differently**.

3 a Read what the radio presenter says about greetings and underline the key words.
How we greet someone for the first time is important because we want people to like us.

b 🔊 1.4 Listen and check.

4 🔊 1.5 Listen to the next part of the radio programme and choose the correct alternatives.
1. Men and women in the US usually *kiss/shake hands* when they meet new people.
2. Men and women in the US sometimes *bow/hug*.
3. Men in Brazil usually *kiss/shake hands*.
4. People in Brazil *sometimes/always* kiss three times.
5. Men and women in Qatar *put their right hand on their chest/shake hands* when they meet.
6. Men in Qatar sometimes *put their hands together/press their noses together*.

5 🔊 1.6 Listen to the last part of the radio programme and complete notes 1–7 with one key word from the box.

| bow | chest | hands | head | high | low | tongue |

South Korea
1. Friends: Bow their _____
2. Business people: _____ with top half of their body
3. Younger people: Bow _____

Thailand
4. Traditional greeting: People put their _____ together and bow their head
5. Friends: Hands are low in front of their _____
6. Older/important people: Hands are _____, fingers near top of their head

Tibet
7. Traditional greeting: People put their hands together and show their _____

6 Work in pairs and discuss the questions.
1. Which greeting in the radio show do you think is the most interesting? Why?
2. Can you think of any other greetings?
3. How do you usually greet the people below?
- family
- friends
- people you don't know
- people you work/study with

1B Develop your writing

> **Goal:** complete a questionnaire
> **Focus:** explaining reasons and results

1 a Work in pairs and discuss the questions.
1. What are the best ways to learn English?
2. What do you use English for?

b Read the questionnaire and match questions 1–6 with gaps A–F.
1. Do you prefer working alone or in pairs/groups?
2. What do you find difficult about learning English?
3. What do you like using to learn English (e.g. books, video, the internet, etc.)?
4. What do you do outside class to practise English?
5. What do you need English for?
6. What do you like doing in class (e.g. listening, speaking, pronunciation, etc.)?

Learning English Questionnaire

Name: *Miguel García*
Teacher: *Diana Norman*

A _____
I need to pass an exam at university. That's why I'm studying English. I think my reading and writing skills are OK, but I really need to improve my speaking for the exam.

B _____
I like having conversations in class because I can't practise speaking English at home. But I also like reading interesting articles, because I can learn new things.

C _____
I like watching videos and I use my phone all the time to look up new words.

D _____
I like working with other students so I can practise speaking, but I don't mind working on my own.

E _____
Pronunciation is the hardest thing for me because of all the different sounds in English.

F _____
When I'm at home I like watching TV programmes in English. I prefer watching them in the original language because I learn a lot of new vocabulary this way.

2 Read the questionnaire again. Decide if the sentences are true (T) or false (F).
1. Miguel has finished university.
2. He doesn't often speak English outside class.
3. He likes working in pairs or groups.
4. He finds it difficult to pronounce words correctly.
5. He learns English while doing something he enjoys at home.

3 Read the Focus box. Then underline the phrases Miguel uses to give examples in the questionnaire.

Explaining reasons and results

Use *because* (*of*) and *so that* to give reasons.
*I was late for class **because** I missed the bus.*
*I couldn't sleep **because of** the noisy traffic.*
*I'm saving money **so that** I can go to University.*
Use *that's why* to explain a result.
*I missed the bus. **That's why** I was late for class.*
*I want to learn new vocabulary - **that's why** I watch TV in English.*

4 Match the sentence halves.
1. I like using social media because
2. I would like to move to the UK. That's why
3. I try to learn ten new words every day, so that
4. I find reading the most difficult skill, because of

a. I can quickly improve my vocabulary.
b. I can chat with people in English from all over the world.
c. all the new words.
d. I'm interested in British English.

5 Choose the correct alternatives.
1. I like listening to songs in English *so that/that's why* I can learn fun words.
2. I need to practise writing emails *because/so that* it's important for my work.
3. I like working in groups *because/because of* the people I meet.
4. I find listening difficult. *Because/That's why* I need to practise it more in class.
5. I would like to have more homework *because of/so that* I can practise at home.

Prepare

6 You're going to answer the questions in Exercise 1b. First, make notes about each one.

Write

7 Write your answers to the questions. Use the Focus box and the Useful phrases to help you.

Useful phrases
I need English for (my job/an exam/my studies).
I really enjoy (speaking in class).
I don't mind (doing exercises for homework), but I prefer (doing online research).
It's difficult to (pronounce some words).

1c Develop your reading

> **Goal:** understand a short article
> **Focus:** reading for specific information

1 Read the title and introduction to the news article. How has Morris recorded his life?

A LIFE IN PHOTOS

Over the past few years, Morris Villarroel from Madrid has recorded everything in his life using a special camera and making lots of notes.

It started in 2010, when he decided to record what happened to him by writing things down in a notebook. He enjoyed it so much that, in 2014, he started taking photos every 30 seconds. He uses a small camera that he carries on his body and it takes about 1,200 photos every day. Most of them aren't very interesting – for example, a picture of his breakfast or his hands when he's driving, but he doesn't delete any of them.

As well as the photos, he has 245 notebooks with his thoughts and ideas inside. He reads his notes regularly to check them.

This sounds strange to a lot of people. Even Morris says that he hasn't seen all of his photos, but he feels it's important to keep a record of his life so that he can look at it when he's older and see what it was like – just like a personal diary. He also wants to create a collection of thoughts and activities to give to his son, who was born at 4.36 p.m. on 4th November, 2014. While most fathers have a few photos of mother and child, Morris recorded the whole day and then every day of his life so far. He hopes that when his son is older he can look back and see what his mother looked like on the day he was born, as well as every day after that.

2 Read the Focus box. What are some examples of specific information?

Reading for specific information

When reading, you often only need to understand specific pieces of information.

Before reading, think about the type of information you need. If you want to know a date, look for a number. If you're looking for a name, then capital letters will help you find it.

Elvis Presley was born in Tupelo, Mississippi, on 8th January 1935.

It also helps to think about where in the text the information will be – at the beginning, in the middle or at the end.

3 a Read the text and answer the questions.
  1 How many photos does Morris take every day?
  2 When did he start recording things?
  3 What time was his son born?
  4 What's Morris's surname?
  5 How often does he take photos?

 b What do you think of Morris's project? Would you like to do something like this?

4 a Read the title and introduction to the text below. Are you interested in this kind of film?

LIFE IN A DAY

In 2010, film-maker Kevin Macdonald asked people from all over the world to spend a day filming their lives. He then edited their videos into a film called *Life in a Day*.

In total, he asked 80,000 people from 192 countries. To make sure he had videos from lots of different countries, Kevin sent out 400 cameras to people in poorer places. They all made their films on 24th July 2010.

He asked people to answer three questions during their films: *What do you love? What do you fear?* and *What's in your pocket?* Kevin directed the film, and he worked closely with Ridley Scott as producer. In the end, they made a film that's 94 minutes and 53 seconds long – from *4,500 hours* of original videos! It was a lot of work.

The film starts with people waking up in the morning, and continues through the day, until night. It shows people with very different lifestyles from all over the world. It was first shown at the Sundance Film Festival in 2011 and, later that year, YouTube made it free to watch on their website.

 b Find the following information in the text.
  1 The name of the producer.
  2 The day people made their films.
  3 The number of people that were asked to make films.
  4 Where you can watch the film for free.
  5 The length of the film.

5 Work in pairs. Talk about a typical day in your life.

2A Develop your reading

> **Goal:** understand a short story
> **Focus:** narrative structure

1. Work in pairs. What kind of stories do you like reading (e.g. adventure, romantic, traditional)? What do you like about them?

2. Read the Focus box. How many parts does a traditional story usually have?

Narrative structure

Many traditional stories follow a similar structure:
- A **Background:** stories usually begin by talking about where and when things are happening, as well as who the important people in the story are.
  A long time ago, there was a mother duck with lots of baby ducks.
- B **Problem(s):** then the story changes, often because something bad or unlucky happens.
  One of the baby ducks was very ugly, and the other baby ducks laughed at him.
- C **Solution(s):** to make sure the story is interesting, there is a solution to the problem.
  When they all grew up, the ugly baby duck became a beautiful swan.
- D **Conclusion:** this is the message of the story.
  Don't treat people differently because of how they look.

Use expressions such as *a long time ago, one night, the next day, a week later* to help structure a story.

---

3. Read the whole story and match paragraphs 1–6 with parts A–D in the Focus box. There is more than one problem and solution in the story.

4. a Read paragraphs 1–3 of the story again and answer the questions.
   1. Where is the story set?
   2. Who are the important people in the story?
   3. Which animals were important to them?
   4. What's the problem in paragraph 2?
   5. Was the old man sad about it?
   6. What happened when the horse returned?
   7. Did the old man think it was good luck?

   b Read paragraphs 4–6 of the story again and answer the questions.
   1. What's the problem in paragraph 4?
   2. Did the old man think it was bad luck?
   3. Why did the army come into the village?
   4. Why didn't they take the old man's son?

5. Work in groups. Do you agree with what the old man says in the last paragraph of the story? Why/Why not?

The old MAN and his HORSE

[1] A long time ago in ancient China, there was an old farmer who lived with his son in a small village in the countryside. He loved his son more than anything in the world. They worked together every day on the farm and rode their horses. They loved their horses very much.

[2] One night, one of the horses ran away. When the people in their village heard that the horse was missing, they came to the old man and said 'We're so sorry about your bad luck!' However, the old man wasn't sad about it. 'There was nothing we could do', said the old man, 'so don't be sad. It wasn't bad luck. It just happened.' The people in the village were surprised and went away.

[3] The next day, the horse came back, bringing with it another white horse. This was a beautiful horse, worth a lot of money. When the people in the village saw this, they were happy for the old man and talked about his good luck. But the old man said, 'It wasn't good luck. It just happened.'

[4] The old man's son loved the new horse and rode it every day. But one day, he fell off the horse and broke his leg. Once again, the people in the village said to the old man 'We're sorry about your bad luck!' The old man replied in the same way as before, 'It wasn't bad luck or the horse's fault. You shouldn't feel sad about what happened.'

[5] A week later, a war started and the army came into the village. They said that every young man should join the army and fight in the war. However, because the old man's son had a broken leg, they decided he could not join the army.

[6] The old man explained to his son, 'When people think you have bad luck, the end result can sometimes be positive, so you shouldn't be too sad. In the same way, when people think you have good luck, you should be careful not to become too happy.'

89

2B Develop your writing

> **Goal:** write a story
> **Focus:** using adverbs to describe actions

1. Work in pairs. Have any of the things below ever happened to you? What happened? How did you feel?
   - you called someone by the wrong name
   - you took something that isn't yours by mistake
   - you missed a bus, train or plane
   - you sent a message to the wrong person

2. Read the story *Taking the biscuit* and answer the questions.
   1. Which situation in Exercise 1 does it describe?
   2. Whose were the biscuits on the table?
   3. How did the woman and the man feel during the train journey?

TAKING THE BISCUIT

It all started when a businessperson bought a coffee, a packet of biscuits and a newspaper, and got on a busy train. She quickly found an empty seat and put her things on the table. She took off her coat, put her handbag carefully on the floor, and sat down. Then she opened her newspaper and started to read.

The young man sitting opposite her was looking at his phone. After half an hour, he calmly and quietly opened the packet of biscuits on the table and took one. The woman couldn't believe it — they were her biscuits! She looked at him angrily, but he just looked back at his phone. So she picked up her coffee, and took a biscuit herself. The man looked up at her and then looked away. After a minute or two, he took another biscuit, and she did the same. This continued until there was only one biscuit left.

Just before the next station, the woman got up slowly, and put her coat on. She took the final biscuit, put it into her mouth, and smiled at the man. He watched her, but he didn't say anything. Then she picked up her handbag, turned around, and got off the train. On the platform, she opened her bag to get out her train ticket. Inside was her unopened packet of biscuits.

3. Read the Focus box. Then find two more adverbs which describe actions in the story.

Using adverbs to describe actions

Use adverbs like *angrily*, *calmly*, *quickly* and *slowly* to describe how an action happens. They help the reader imagine the events in a story. Adverbs are usually formed by adding *-ly* to the end of adjectives.
*She got up **slowly**.*
They can come before or after the verb.
*She **quickly** found an empty seat.*
*She looked at him **angrily**.*
Some adjectives have irregular adverbs.
fast – fast
good – well

4. a Complete the man's story with the adverbs in the box. Sometimes more than one answer is possible.

   | angrily   calmly   carefully   quickly   quietly   slowly |

   I ¹_____ put my coffee and biscuits on the table in the train. After a while, I opened the packet and took one. The woman who sat down opposite me looked at me ²_____. I didn't know why, so I looked back down at my mobile phone and ³_____ ate my biscuit. Then the woman ⁴_____ took one of my biscuits and ate it. I was really surprised! We each continued to take one biscuit at a time, and eat them ⁵_____. We didn't say a word to each other. Just before the next stop, she stood up and ⁶_____ took the last one. So strange!

   b Work in pairs and compare your answers. Do you agree with each other's choice of adverbs?

Prepare

5. a You're going to write a story about something that happened to you. It can be real or imagined. First, answer the questions below and make notes.
   - Where did the story happen?
   - When did it happen?
   - Who is in the story?
   - Did something good/bad/funny happen?
   - What happened in the end?
   - How did you feel?

   b Write down any verbs and adverbs you can use in your story.

Write

6. a Write your story. Use your notes in Exercise 5 and the story in Exercise 2 to help you.

   b Work in pairs and read each other's stories. Which adverbs did your partner use in their story?

2c Develop your listening

> **Goal:** understand a short talk
> **Focus:** recognising weak forms

1 Look at the photos. Which dishes would you most/least like to eat?

2 a 🔊 **2.9** Listen to the introduction to a radio show. What's it called? What's the topic this week?

 b 🔊 **2.10** Listen to Jenny and Sara present their ideas. Decide if the statements are true (T) or false (F).
1 Jenny thinks meat doesn't taste nice.
2 Jenny thinks you should never eat meat.
3 Jenny thinks there are many problems with eating meat.
4 Sara thinks farming insects is cheap.
5 Sara thinks eating insects can help the world.
6 Sara thinks insects don't taste nice.

3 Read the Focus box. Which words are usually pronounced in their weak form?

Recognising weak forms
Important words in a sentence are usually stressed. The words that have less meaning (e.g. articles, auxiliary verbs and prepositions) aren't stressed and are usually pronounced in their weak form.

Welcome to this week's episode of 'What a great idea!' – the show that gives you a lot to think about.

Recognising weak forms is important so you can understand natural speech.

4 a 🔊 **2.11** Underline the weak forms in the extracts. Then listen and check.
1 I love it, and I ate it all the time.
2 I decided to make a change.
3 It's good for us to eat less meat if we can.
4 We need to move the meat from place to place.
5 It's a lot cheaper of course.
6 I always thought that vegetarian food was boring.

 b 🔊 **2.12** Listen and complete the extracts with the weak forms.
1 I think it's a good idea _____ everyone to eat insects.
2 People eat _____ as a basic food.
3 The reason is _____ insects are actually very good for us.
4 They're great _____ add to our diets.
5 Insects _____ help us to feed everyone.
6 There are thousands _____ different kinds of insects.

5 🔊 **2.13** Listen to the discussion between the presenter and Jenny and Sara. Answer the questions.
1 When does Jenny think a good time to eat meat is?
2 Does she think that we should never eat meat more than two days a week?
3 Why does Sara think some people don't like the idea of eating insects?

6 Work in groups and discuss the questions.
1 Do you agree that it's a good idea to not eat meat for five days a week? Why/Why not?
2 Do you think that eating insects is a good idea? Why/Why not?

91

3A Develop your reading

> **Goal:** understand a factual text
> **Focus:** guessing the meaning of words

1 Read the text. How many different parts are there to Superkilen?

SUPERKILEN a park for the people

What do you do when you want to improve an old part of town where lots of different people live? City planners in Denmark have the answer.

Superkilen opened in June 2012 because they wanted to make the area cleaner and more interesting than it was before. The park is half a mile long and is in the Nørrebro district of Copenhagen. People in the area come from all over the world, and the park shows their different **backgrounds**. Many of the **features** in the park are from different countries, for example the bins are from the UK and there are lovely **benches** from Brazil for people to sit on and enjoy the nice views.

The park has three parts: Red Square, Black Market and Green Park. Red Square is painted red, pink and orange, and local people go there to have fun and do activities like riding a bike around the cycle **track**. Black Market is a traditional town square and is busier than Red Square. People use it as a meeting place and have barbecues here. In the middle of the square there's a **fountain** from Morocco – when it lights up at night the water looks beautiful. Green Park, where everything is completely green, is longer than the other parts of Superkilen and has lots of hills, trees and flowers. People like having picnics, doing sports and walking their dogs in this part of the park.

With features from all over the world and people from so many different countries, Superkilen has a really international feel to it.

2 Read the text again and answer the questions.
1. How old is Superkilen?
2. Which city is it in?
3. Where do the people in the area come from?
4. Is Red Square or Black Market more popular?
5. What is special about Green Park?

3 Read the Focus box. How can we understand words that we don't know in a text?

Guessing the meaning of words

When you find a word that you don't understand in a text, you can often use the information around it to guess its meaning. For example:
*The park ... is in the Nørrebro **district** of Copenhagen.*
The phrase before *district* tells you where the park is and you can understand that Nørrebro is the name of a place in Copenhagen. From this information, you can guess that *district* means *area* or *part of a city*.

4 Work in pairs. Try to guess the meaning of the words in bold in the Superkilen text. Choose the correct alternatives.
1. backgrounds: *people's family and education etc./a large number of people*
2. features: *people who go to parks/things you find in a place*
3. benches: *things to look at/things to sit on*
4. track: *a type of path/a shop*
5. fountain: *a thing with moving water/a type of tree*

5 Read about Metropol Parasol. What can you do there?

METROPOL PARASOL
A MIX OF OLD AND NEW

Metropol Parasol in Seville is a very popular place for both locals and tourists. But the original plans for the area were very different.

In 1990, people started building a huge underground car park in La Encarnación square in the old town. But when they began, workers on the project found a major **obstacle** in the way. They found some ancient **ruins** under the square, so work had to stop. However, in 2004, city planners had an idea – use the ruins to make a museum, then build a space above it for people to enjoy.

Designed by German architect Jürgen Mayer, Metropol Parasol is a wooden building with four levels. Level 0 is an underground museum with the ancient ruins. Level 1 has a street market – this is a popular meeting place for local people, especially because there is a lot of **shade** from the sun during the hot summer months. Levels 2 and 3 are open areas where you can go to restaurants, go for a walk or simply enjoy **stunning** views of the city.

The design of the building was **inspired by** the shape of the underground rooms in the Cathedral of Seville as well as the trees in a local Seville square. There really is no other park like it in the world – it's completely **unique**. So if you ever visit Seville, don't miss Metropol Parasol.

6 a Write down what you think the words in bold in the text in Exercise 5 mean.

b Work in pairs and compare your ideas. Then check in a dictionary.

7 Work in pairs. Which park would you most like to visit? Why?

3B Develop your writing

> **Goal:** write a hotel review
>
> **Focus:** organising ideas

1. Have you ever written a review? What was it for?

2. a Read the review. What is it for?

◉◉◉◉◐ Reviewed 30th July

We stayed at the Hotel Alpine for a week in June. It's one of the most beautiful places I've ever visited. You can walk through forests or around the lake. It's really peaceful, but the birds can be quite noisy!

Our room was comfortable and a good size. The cleaners came only twice during the week but that wasn't really a problem. There was wifi in the room and it worked well most days. There's a pool, a sauna and a gym in the hotel. I didn't use them but other guests said they were small but good. There's a nice restaurant and breakfast is included in the price. Dinner was good and quite cheap, too. The chef's special was always delicious but there wasn't a lot of choice for vegetarians.

The main problem with this hotel is transport. There's a supermarket, some shops and a couple of restaurants a ten-minute drive away but it takes 30 minutes without a car. We rented a car so we were OK but other guests found it more difficult. Another problem is the noise from the road. Unfortunately, it's very busy all the time so it's a good idea to ask for a room on the south side where it's quieter.

Before you decide to stay at this hotel, it's good to ask yourself two questions. Do you want a relaxing holiday with lots of fresh air? Do you have a car? If the answer is 'yes' to both, then this hotel is a great choice.

b Read the review again and answer the questions.
1. What positive and negative things does the writer say about the topics in the box?

| food | sports facilities | the area | the room |
| the wifi | transport | | |

2. What two recommendations does the writer give?
3. What's the main topic in each paragraph?

3. Read the Focus box. Why is it important to organise your ideas?

Organising ideas
It's important to organise your ideas well so your readers can follow them clearly. For example, in a review of a hotel, you could organise your ideas like this:
1. Where, when, who with
   We stayed at the Hotel Alpine for a week in June.
2. General information/positive things
   Our room was comfortable and a good size.
3. Any problems
   The main problem with this hotel is transport.
4. Recommendation
   If the answer is 'yes' to both, then this hotel is a great choice.

4. Organise the ideas below into categories 1–4 in the Focus box.
   - friendly staff
   - hotel in excellent sailing area
   - stayed for two weeks in summer
   - best hotel - everyone should go there
   - big, comfortable rooms
   - great restaurant
   - beach really busy in the morning
   - went on sailing holiday to France with family

Prepare
5. a Think about a hotel you've stayed in. Make notes about the positive and negative things for each topic below.
   - the area
   - the rooms
   - the facilities
   - the restaurant/food
   - transport
   - things to do

   b Choose two things to write about for each topic.

   c Decide how to organise your review. Use the categories in the Focus box to help you.

Write
6. Write your review. Use the Useful phrases to help you.

   Useful phrases
   I stayed at (Hotel Majestic) for (seven) days.
   My room was (comfortable/clean/a good size).
   The staff were (friendly/rude).
   The main problem was that (it was too hot).
   If you like (quiet places), this is a great hotel for you.

3c Develop your listening

> **Goal:** understand an interview
> **Focus:** predicting information

3 Read the Focus box. What three things can help us predict what someone will say?

Predicting information
When people listen they often naturally predict what they think they will hear next. You can use your knowledge of the topic, the situation and the speaker to guess what you think you will hear.

For example, if you're listening to a radio interview about someone who climbed a mountain, you can predict that they will talk about who they went with, how long it took and any problems they had.

When listening, try to predict what you will hear to help you focus.

4 🔊 3.10 Predict the reasons Karen will give for her plan. Then listen to the next part of the interview and check your ideas.

5 a Karen talks about the three places below. Write some words or phrases you think she will use for each one.
1 The Great Wall of China *long*
2 Iceland
3 Mount Kilimanjaro

b 🔊 3.11 Listen and check your answers. Did Karen use any of the words you predicted?

c Listen again and answer the questions.
1 How far along The Great Wall did Karen walk?
2 How did she describe some of the places there?
3 Why didn't she see the Northern Lights?
4 What did she do instead?
5 Why did she want to climb Mount Kilimanjaro?
6 Why didn't she feel well?

6 a You're going to listen to Karen talk about learning to fly and going on a safari holiday. Why do you think she wants to do these things?

b 🔊 3.12 Listen and check your predictions.

c Listen again and answer the questions.
1 Why isn't flying a plane going to be easy for Karen?
2 Why does she want to learn to fly?
3 Where does she want to go on safari?
4 Which animals does she want to see?
5 Why does she want see the animals on safari?

7 Work in groups and discuss the questions.
1 What amazing experiences would you like to have in your life?
2 Would you like to do the same things as Karen?

1 a Match the activities in the box with photos A–D.

climb Mount Kilimanjaro   go on a safari holiday
learn to fly   see the Northern Lights
walk along the Great Wall of China

b Work in pairs and discuss the questions.
1 Do you know anyone who has done the activities in Exercise 1a?
2 Would you like to do any of the activities? Why/Why not?

2 🔊 3.9 Listen to the introduction to a radio interview. What's Karen's plan?

4A Develop your writing

> **Goal:** write and respond to an invitation
>
> **Focus:** inviting and responding

1 a Read Chris and Lily's invitation. What's it for?

> **Come and celebrate with us!**
> Lily and I are going to celebrate our birthdays together this year – we're having a dinner for all our friends at our house on 26th June. There'll be food, music and a few games, too.
> We'd love you to come and have fun with us!
> Our address is 26A Station Road and dinner is at 7 p.m. (but feel free to come any time after 6). Children are welcome, so please bring them!
> Please let us know if you can come by 10th June.
> We hope you can make it.
> Chris and Lily

b Read the invitation again. What time can people come to their house?

2 Read the Focus box. What phrases can you use to respond to an invitation?

> **Inviting and responding**
> You can use some specific phrases when you write an invitation in English.
> *We'd love you to come.*
> *We hope you can make it.*
> You can also use similar phrases when responding to an invitation.
> *We'd love to come.*
> *Of course we'll be there!*
> If you can't accept an invitation, it's always a good idea to say why and use expressions like *but, unfortunately, I'm afraid* and *have fun/a great time* to be polite.
> *Sorry, but unfortunately we can't make it. We're on holiday then.*
> *I'm afraid I can't come - it's my sister's birthday. Have a great time!*

3 a Read the replies to Chris and Lily's invitation. Who can come?

> Sue Watts
> Thanks for inviting us, we'd love to come. Could you tell us the best way to get to your house? Do you want us to bring anything?
> Sue and Phil

> Henrick Souza
> Hi Chris and Lily,
> I'm afraid I can't come on the 26th. I'm going to be away on a business trip that week. I'll think of you all though. Have fun while I work hard!

b Read the replies again and answer the questions.
1. What phrase do Sue and Phil use to accept?
2. What two things do they ask?
3. What phrase does Henrick use to say *no*?
4. What reason does he give?

4 Read another invitation and the replies. Choose the correct alternatives.

> Dear friends,
> It's my 30th birthday next month, and I've decided to have a party. I'd ¹*love/want* to see you there.
> It's going to be at my house on 7th September. It will start at around 7 p.m., and there's going be lots of music and dancing!
> Let me know if you need any more details. I hope you can all ²*do/make it*!
> Best wishes,
> Jonathan

> Hi Jonathan,
> Wow, 30 already? I can't believe it! ³*I'd/I* love to come, but ⁴*badly/unfortunately* it's the same day as my friend's wedding. Have a ⁵*great/big* time and let's do something when you get back.
> Suzanne

> Hi Jonathan,
> Fantastic news! Of course ⁶*we/we'll* be there. It's going to be the party of the century!
> Do you want us to bring anything?
> Marsha and James

Prepare

5 You're going to invite people to an event. First, make notes about the things below:
- what the event is
- what will happen at it
- the location
- the time
- if people need to bring anything
- any other important information

Write

6 a Write your invitation.

b Work in pairs. Read each other's invitations and write a reply to accept.

c Work in different pairs. Read each other's invitations and write a reply to say you can't come.

4B Develop your listening

> **Goal:** understand instructions
> **Focus:** sequencing words

1 Work in pairs. Look at the photos and discuss the questions.
1 Do you use any apps to help you in these places?
2 What other apps do you use regularly?

2 a 🔊 4.4 Listen to Alicia and Jake talking about two apps, Buzz Tree and Eventroots. What does each app do?

b Listen again. Decide if the statements below refer to Buzz Tree (B) or Eventroots (E).
1 You add where the event will be.
2 You enter information about what you like.
3 It gives you ideas about places to go.
4 You can invite people from your contacts.
5 It shows you who's coming.

3 Read the Focus box. Do you know any other sequencing words?

Sequencing words

When people give instructions, they often use sequencing words (*first*, *next*, etc.) to introduce each stage (start, middle or end) of the instructions. These words help the listener follow the conversation.
First, type in your name.
Next/After that, it asks you to create a password.
Finally, press 'invite', and you're finished!
Try to listen for sequencing words so that you can follow instructions better.

4 a 🔊 4.5 Listen and underline the sequencing words you hear.
1 *First/Next*, you answer some questions about you.
2 *Next/After that* you press 'Go'.
3 And *then/finally* it gives you ideas for things to do.
4 Well, *finally/to start with*, you add the details in this box here.
5 *Next/Then*, you invite people by adding their email addresses.
6 *First/After that*, people can reply and say if they can come or not.
7 *Finally/Then* you can update the event.

b Complete the table with the sequencing words in Exercise 4a.

start	middle	end
First		

5 a 🔊 4.6 Listen to someone explaining how to use another app and number stages a–f in the correct order.
a The person can see your location.
b Download the Famsafe app. *1*
c Share your location with that person.
d Turn on GPS.
e If something happens, you can send an emergency message.
f Find someone in your contacts.

b Listen again and complete the extracts.
1 _____ , make sure you have GPS turned on, like this.
2 _____ find me in your contacts.
3 _____ , select 'share my location with this user'.
4 _____ , when I open the app I can see where you are in real time.
5 _____ , if you need to call me in an emergency, just say 'call Mum' and your phone will call me.

6 Work in pairs and discuss the questions.
1 What's your favourite app? What's it for? How often do you use it?
2 Do you use any apps you think other people might not know about?

96

4C Develop your reading

› **Goal:** understand a review
› **Focus:** understanding pronouns

1 Read the advert. What's a *bootcamp*?

2 Read reviews A–C and match them with headings 1–3.
   1 Not very relaxing
   2 A weekend to repeat
   3 Everyone was helpful

3 Read the Focus box. Can you think of any other examples of pronouns?

Understanding pronouns

We use pronouns (e.g. *she, it, they, this, that*, etc.) in a text when we don't want to repeat a word, phrase or sentence. This makes the text sound better.

Last year I went to a bootcamp. The staff there were strict but kind. They gave me a lot of help. It was actually a lot of fun and this surprised me.

It's important to understand which word or phrase a pronoun refers to so that we can read texts more quickly.

They = The staff
It = bootcamp
this = a lot of fun

4 a Look at the words in bold in review A. What does each one refer to? Choose the correct option, a or b.
   1 it: **a** the farmhouse   **b** the countryside
   2 this: **a** guests have their own room
          b guests share a bathroom
   3 it: **a** other guests are tidy   **b** sharing a bathroom
   4 it: **a** have a great time   **b** go to the boot camp

  b Find pronouns in reviews B and C that refer to:
   1 noise
   2 building a bigger gym
   3 a wedding ring
   4 a mobile phone and TV

5 Read the reviews again and answer the questions.
Which reviewer(s) A–C …
   1 liked the evening activities?
   2 didn't expect to share a bathroom?
   3 had good things to say about the trainers?
   4 plans to go to the bootcamp again in the future?
   5 felt good after doing the bootcamp?
   6 wants to continue doing one of the activities in future?
   7 had to do an activity in an unusual place?
   8 almost lost something important?

6 Work in groups and discuss the questions.
   1 Would you like to go to a bootcamp? Why/Why not?
   2 Why do you think people like going to bootcamps?

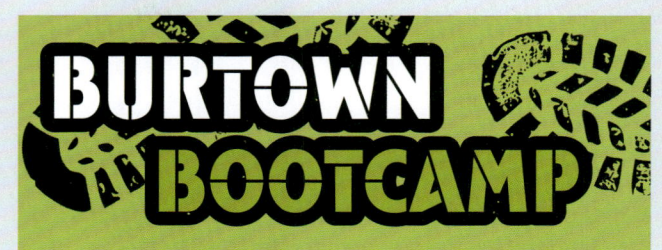

BURTOWN BOOTCAMP

› **DO YOU WANT TO GET FIT?**
› **DO YOU WANT TO CHALLENGE YOURSELF?**

Then come and spend a weekend with our excellent trainers. Spend two days running, walking and exercising in the gym, as well as lots of other fun activities! It doesn't matter if you can run only 20 metres or if you often run 20 km — we can help you get fitter. Stay in our beautiful farmhouse and enjoy the countryside around you. You'll leave feeling healthier and more relaxed.

A
I really enjoyed myself at the bootcamp. The farmhouse is big and very pretty and the countryside around ¹**it** is beautiful. Guests have their own room but they have to share a bathroom. I didn't know ²**this** when I booked the weekend so I was surprised and a bit angry when I arrived. However, ³**it** was actually OK because the other guests were tidy. The activities were enjoyable and I felt much better when I left. I really enjoyed the clean, fresh air. It wasn't a cheap weekend away but I had a great time so I'm going to do ⁴**it** again.

B
I was unhappy with the weekend. I have a very stressful job in the city so I really needed some peace and quiet. They were building a bigger gym when I was there, so there was a lot of noise all of the time. It was really loud. Also, this meant that we had to do a lot of the classes in the car park instead of the gym, which wasn't very relaxing. It was a bit of a shame because the trainers were great and I especially liked the team games after dinner. So, I enjoyed being out of the city and away from my computer, but I needed a stress-free weekend and it wasn't stress-free at all.

C
I enjoyed the weekend. The trainers gave me lots of ideas and the chef cooked vegetarian meals especially for me. They weren't always the nicest meals but they were healthy. On the second day, my wedding ring fell off in the forest. I was so worried! But all the staff and guests were lovely and helped me find it. The bedrooms are fine but I didn't know that we had to share bathrooms. You can't use your mobile phone or watch TV, either. I talked to other people more without them, so maybe it was a good thing. I felt heathier at the end of the two days, and that's what I wanted. I'm going to do yoga every day now!

5A Develop your reading

> **Goal:** understand an article
> **Focus:** identifying positive and negative points

1 a Work in pairs. Do you think technology is making our working lives easier or more difficult? Why?

  b Read the article and compare your ideas with those in the text.

2 Match the headings A–E with paragraphs 1–4 in the article. There is one extra heading that you don't need.
  A Communication problems
  B Faster but busier
  C In control of our time
  D Technology and health
  E Too much time at home?

3 Read the Focus box. Then underline the phrases that introduce positive and negative points in the first paragraph of the article.

Identifying positive and negative points

Articles often include both positive and negative sides to an argument.
Look for key words and phrases to help you decide if an idea is positive or negative.

Positive
It's good that …
This has one main advantage …
The main benefit is that …

Negative
It's difficult to …
One problem is …
It's not good that …

You can also use the linking words *however* and *but* to introduce opposite ideas.
However, is this really true?

4 a Read the article again and answer the questions.
   What are the positive and negative points about …
   1 working anywhere and at any time?
   2 working from home?
   3 working in international teams?
   4 sharing information?

  b Work in pairs. Which language in the article helped you decide if a point is positive or negative?

Technology in the workplace: a help or not?

Technology is changing fast and work is changing with it. For some people these changes are positive but for others they are not. We had a look at four ways in which our working lives have changed because of new technology

1 _____
Technology helps us to work anywhere at any time and this has one main advantage – we can choose the hours we want to work. We don't have to start and finish work at a specific time like our parents did. We can start late when we want to do some exercise first. We can start early and finish early when we have to pick up the children from school. We can pay more attention to our social lives. However is this really true? With a smartphone in our hands, we're always available. It's difficult to find time for ourselves because we take our work with us. Think about that next time you're reading a work email on a beach in Spain.

2 _____
More and more people work from home these days. This means that workers don't see their colleagues as much. This is good when you prefer to work in a quiet place, but it's bad if you don't like spending time too much on your own. Of course, there are other advantages. People spend less time travelling to and from work and companies save money by having smaller offices. Is work only about money though?

3 _____
In the past, meetings with people in other countries were only possible after long journeys. Today, people regularly work in international teams and meet online. The main benefit of this is that people in the company can work together easily and cheaply. But online meetings can sometimes have problems. It can be difficult to hear when people speak quietly or at the same time. The internet connection can often be bad, too. Sometimes it's better to get on a plane and meet face-to-face!

4 _____
Technology helps us to find and share information really fast these days. We can work more quickly because we don't have to wait for hours or even days for information to arrive. The problem is that it's so easy to share information, our email inboxes are often completely full. We spend most of our working life reading and responding to these messages. When do we have time to actually do some work?